CONTEMPORARY WRITERS

General Editors
MALCOLM BRADBURY
and
CHRISTOPHER BIGSBY

SAUL BELLOW

SAUL
BELLOW

MALCOLM BRADBURY

METHUEN
LONDON AND NEW YORK

First published in 1982 by
Methuen & Co. Ltd
11 New Fetter Lane, London EC4P 4EE
Published in the USA by
Methuen & Co.
in association with Methuen, Inc.
733 Third Avenue, New York, NY 10017

Typeset by Rowland Phototypesetting Ltd
Printed in Great Britain by
Richard Clay (The Chaucer Press) Ltd
Bungay, Suffolk

British Library Cataloguing in Publication Data

Bradbury, Malcolm
Saul Bellow. – (Contemporary writers)
1. Bellow, Saul – Criticism and interpretation.
I. Title   II. Series
813'.52   PS3503.E4488Z/

ISBN 0-416-31650-6

Library of Congress Cataloging in Publication Data

Bradbury, Malcolm.
Saul Bellow.
(Contemporary writers)
Bibliography: p.
1. Bellow, Saul – Criticism and interpretation.
I. Title   II. Series.
PS3503.E4488ZXOX   1982   813'.52   81-22500
ISBN 0-416-31650-6 (pbk.)   AACR2

For Edmond Schraepen,
in memory
and lasting affection

CONTENTS

GENERAL EDITORS' PREFACE

Over the past twenty years or so, it has become clear that a decisive change has taken place in the spirit and character of contemporary writing. There now exists around us, in fiction, drama and poetry, a major achievement which belongs to our experience, our doubts and uncertainties, our ways of perceiving – an achievement stylistically radical and novel, and likely to be regarded as quite as exciting, important and innovative as that of any previous period. This is a consciousness and a confidence that has grown very slowly. In the 1950s it seemed that, somewhere amidst the dark realities of the Second World War, the great modernist impulse of the early years of this century had exhausted itself, and that the post-war arts would be arts of recessiveness, pale imitation, relative sterility. Some, indeed, doubted the ability of literature to survive the experiences of holocaust. A few major figures seemed to exist, but not a style or a direction. By the 1960s the confidence was greater, the sense of an avant-garde returned, the talents multiplied, and there was a growing hunger to define the appropriate styles, tendencies and forms of a new time. And by the 1970s it was not hard to see that we were now surrounded by a remarkable, plural, innovative generation, indeed several layers of generations, whose works represented a radical inquiry into contemporary forms and required us to read and understand – or, often, to read and *not* understand – in quite new ways. Today, as the 1980s start, that cumulative post-war achievement has acquired a degree of coherence that allows for critical response and understanding; hence the present series.

We thus start it in the conviction that the age of Beckett, Borges, Nabokov, Bellow, Pynchon, Robbe-Grillet, Golding, Murdoch, Fowles, Grass, Handke and Calvino, of Albee, Mamet, Shepard, Ionesco, Orton, Pinter and Stoppard, of Ginsberg, Lowell, Ashbery, Paz, Larkin and Hughes, and many another, is indeed an outstanding age of international creation, striking experiment, and some degree of aesthetic coherence. It is a time that has been described as 'post-modern', in the sense that it is an era consequent to modernism yet different from it, having its own distinctive preoccupations and stylistic choices. That term has its limitations, because it is apt to generate too precise definitions of the contemporary experiment, and has acquired rather too specific associations with contemporary American writing; but it does help concentrate our sense of living in a distinctive period. With the new writing has come a new criticism or rather a new critical theorem, its thrust being 'structuralist' or 'deconstructive' – a theorem that not only coexists with but has affected that writing (to the point where many of the best theorists write fictions, the best fictionalists write criticism). Again, its theory can be hermetic and enclosing, if not profoundly apocalyptic; but it points to the presence in our time of a new sense of the status of word and text, author and reader, which shapes and structures the making of modern form.

The aim of 'Contemporary Writers' is to consider some of the most important figures in this scene, looking from the standpoint of and at the achievement of the writers themselves. Its aims are eclectic, and it will follow no tight definition of the contemporary; it will function on the assumption that contemporary writing is by its nature multidirectional and elusive, since styles and directions keep constantly changing in writers who, unlike the writers of the past, are continuous, incomplete, not dead (though several of these studies will address the careers of those who, though dead, remain our contemporaries, as many of those who continue to write are manifestly not). A fair criticism of living writers must be assertive but also provisional, just as a fair sense of contemporary style must be open to that most crucial of contemporary awarenesses, that of the suddenness of change. We do not assume, then, that there is one right path to contemporary experiment, nor that a self-conscious reflexiveness, a deconstructive strategy, an art of performance or a metafictional mode is the only one of current importance. As Iris Murdoch said, 'a strong agile realism which is of course not photographic naturalism' – associated perhaps especially with British writing, but also with Latin-American and American – is also a major component of modern style.

So in this series we wish to identify major writers, some of whom are avant-garde, others who are familiar, even popular, but all of whom are in some serious sense contemporary and in some contemporary sense serious. The aim is to offer brief, lucid studies of their work which draw on modern theoretical issues but respond, as much modern criticism does not, to their distinctiveness and individual interest. We have looked for contributors who are engaged with their subjects – some of them being significant practising authors themselves, writing out of creative experience, others of whom are critics whose interest is personal as well as theoretical. Each volume will provide a thorough account of the author's work so far, a solid bibliography, a personal judgement – and, we hope, an enlarged understanding of writers who are important, not only because of the individual force of their work, but because they are ours in ways no past writer could really be.

Norwich, England, 1981   MALCOLM BRADBURY
                                                             CHRISTOPHER BIGSBY

PREFACE AND
ACKNOWLEDGEMENTS

Brief books need clear principles of economy; I had better explain mine. We live in a time when the novel is changing radically, when new aesthetics are emerging and new ways of reading are needed. Saul Bellow, one of the most important of our living novelists, is a writer who has both expressed and reacted against much that is at work in this new mood. This is his proper task as a serious and deeply perceptive contemporary writer. Frank Kermode once said of him that 'he is so good that anybody can see it with half an eye', and that only a severe doctrinal adhesion could make one question that view. Bellow's struggles with and dissents from current fictional tendencies are thus an important story, because he is one of the most intensely intelligent of novelists, both responding to and sifting the great ideas that drive us, and he sees the novel as a fundamental mode of humane enquiry. Humanism is anxiously subscribed to in our time, in a century that has struggled, with notably few successes, to offer forms of higher materialism. Bellow subscribes — all too rhetorically, some would say — to a humanistic, even transcendental, view of man. His fiction is a fiction of struggle, formal and philosophical, and has taken a variety of forms. But it is not hard to see behind it a moral, intellectual and metaphysical undertaking of great and classic power. To some, including myself, his work has come to look both formally and philosophically conservative; the problem is to see what it is he seeks to conserve, and to grasp the scale of

11

the undertaking, for there can be no doubt that his novels are battlegrounds of contemporary intellectual dispositions, encounters with both our potential despair and our possibility.

Bellow is, in short, a novelist of the present tensions, but above all of the comedy, of the human mind as it seeks to bring new meaning to contingency. The comedy is crucial, and it is the comic Bellow, the novelist of high modern absurdities, that I concentrate on here. I shall say almost nothing about his life, not much about his short stories, plays or non-fiction, little about the several excellent critical studies that have helped illuminate his work. I shall concentrate most on those of his novels I think finest, and write personally, wanting to come to terms with a writer who for me has influentially explored so many of the contemporary anxieties of the novel and the underlying struggles behind its present existence.

I began to read Bellow's fiction in the late 1940s – when I was still at school, and when his first two books came out in Britain in courageous editions from the small press of John Lehmann – and found him a writer of extraordinary modern largeness, an intellectual inheritor of our largest thoughts and concerns, a bravura metaphysical stylist who denied the post-war mood of intellectual recession, so conspicuously felt in Britain. His insistence on an intelligent modernity, his cosmopolitanism and his address to the great themes of the earlier twentieth-century novel, helped explain why the post-war American novel offered a new claim on us. His sense that it was in the troubled fate of humanism in lasting struggle with totalist and totalitarian models of the relation between individual and society that the novel now found its direction influenced my own directions as a writer.

I have therefore been writing essays on his work for a long time; this study draws – variously, partially and in a spirit of Bellovian self-argument with earlier ideas – on a number of these: 'Saul Bellow's *The Victim*', *Critical Quarterly*, 5, 2 (Summer 1963), pp. 119–28; 'Saul Bellow and the Naturalist Tradition', *A Review of English Studies*, 4, 4 (October 1963), pp. 80–92; 'Saul Bellow's *Henderson the Rain King*', *The*

Listener, 71, 1818 (30 January 1964), pp. 187–8; 'Saul Bellow's *Herzog*', *Critical Quarterly*, 7, 3 (Autumn 1965), pp. 269–78; 'The It and the We: Saul Bellow's New Novel', *Encounter*, 45, 5 (November 1975), pp. 61–7; 'Saul Bellow and the Nobel Prize', *Journal of American Studies*, 11, 1 (April 1977), pp. 3–12; and ' "The Nightmare in Which I'm Trying to Get a Good Night's Rest": Saul Bellow and Changing History', in Edmond Schraepen (ed.), *Saul Bellow and His Work* (Brussels: Vrije Universiteit Brussel, 1978). I am indebted to the editors of all these journals, and to many friends and students – especially those in the post-modernism seminar – at the University of East Anglia with whom I have discussed Bellow. But especially to Edmond Schraepen. The last-mentioned volume records the proceedings of a major conference organized by him in Brussels, where he held his chair, in 1977; he was a good friend who, shortly after that conference, died young and suddenly. This book is dedicated to him in deepest lasting affection.

Norwich, England, 1981   MALCOLM BRADBURY

A NOTE ON THE TEXTS

Page references for quotations from Saul Bellow's fiction are to the British Penguin editions unless otherwise indicated. The following abbreviations have been used:

DM   *Dangling Man*
V   *The Victim*
AM   *The Adventures of Augie March*
SD   *Seize the Day*
HRK   *Henderson the Rain King*
H   *Herzog*
MM   *Mosby's Memoirs, and Other Stories*
MSP   *Mr Sammler's Planet*
HG   *Humboldt's Gift*
DD   *The Dean's December* (New York: Harper & Row, 1982)
NT   'Some Notes on Recent American Fiction', in M. Bradbury (ed.), *The Novel Today: Writers on Modern Fiction* (London: Fontana, 1977)

1

SAUL BELLOW AND THE CONTEMPORARY NOVEL

A novel is balanced between a few true impressions and the multitude of false ones that make up most of what we call life. It tells us that for every human being there is a diversity of existences, that the single existence is itself an illusion in part, that these many existences signify something, tend to something, fulfill something; it promises us meaning, harmony, and even justice. (Nobel Prize speech)

It is generally agreed that we live in a remarkably fertile but also a highly unstable age of fiction, a period in which the form we have inherited from the empirical bourgeois world of the past has been forced into constant processes of rediscovery. The first half of this century saw an extraordinary reconstitution of the novel as a form, a pattern of structural changes so deep that we are still discovering and grasping their implications. But, somewhere around the breaking point of the Second World War, directions seemed to change yet again. The strength of the generation of writers who began to emerge during and after that war has only slowly become apparent to us; the directions of development still remain difficult to put into any order. But what is clear is that, just as the major novelists of the early twentieth century sought to find in a changed historical world a new aesthetic deliverance, so the same sort of enterprise, the attempt to press the novel onward so that it might be a serious and enlarging penetration of the structure of contemporary human experience, and of the grammars and languages by which we name it into existence, has continued; the novel at its most self-enquiring is vitally alive now.

Yet its directions of development have been remarkably

uncertain. The 1940s and 1950s saw a reaction against two of the dominant streams of the 1930s: the highly aestheticized forms of modernism, the demanding claims of political naturalism. In France the existential novel emerged; in Britain and the United States there was a move toward a new liberal realism, bleakly made, and marked by dark existential and absurdist insights and by moral desires. By the 1960s directions seemed to have changed again: a late twentieth-century form of novel emerged – preoccupied with the status of its own fictionality, with the death of the central subject, with the collapse of realism, the unreality of history and reportage, the failing power of story, and with the nature of its own text and the coming-into-existence of its own making. Absurdism and black humour pushed onward into *chosisme* and reflexiveness; and dehistoricity, fantasy and an art of foregrounded text and self-conscious process came to seem the type of our most enquiring forms of fictional narrative. In these developments it was possible to read an experimental direction affected and shaped by modernism, yet distinguishable from it in many of its features. Writers like Samuel Beckett, Vladimir Nabokov and Jorge Luis Borges took and extended modernist assumptions, which crossed with a new pluri-generic, provisional mood in the youth culture of the 1960s and the intellectual revisionism of an age that felt itself placed beyond the great theoretics of Marx and Freud, to generate a new aesthetic mood. A new stylistic multiplicity – ranging from the minimalism of the French *nouveaux romanciers* to the massive over-registration of writers like Thomas Pynchon, amassing matter to dissolve single meaning; from the magical realism of Latin American writers like Márquez, Cortazar and Carpentier to the metafictionality of authors like John Barth or Italo Calvino – made single definitions hard to reach, as they always are in art; yet they invited a new sense of creation, and a new mode of reading.

The question of whether all this constituted a decisive break with modernism, and whether such inventive changes of direction marked the coming of a new concept of artistic action and form, began to surface in the surrounding debates. Novelistic creation seemed in process of redefinition, and a lore of new beginnings displayed itself. 'The contemporary writer who is acutely in touch with the life of which he is a part – is forced to start from scratch: reality doesn't exist, time doesn't exist, personality doesn't exist', announced one American experimentalist, Ronald Sukenick, in his aptly entitled *The Death of the Novel and Other Stories* (1969), claiming both the end of story and its continuance. Critics, almost everywhere except perhaps in Britain, grew excited. In consequence, two philosophies of the contemporary condition of fiction seem to co-exist and contend with us today. One holds that the twentieth century has indeed seen the exhaustion of that classic bourgeois object, the old novel. Its modes and historical justifications have somehow dissolved, its historical tactics of empiricism and realism are no longer logically presentable, its regimen of structured narrative made out of definable characters and recognizable social behaviours and structures, of historical realities and objects firmly in place, cannot be made to function. We live in some cruel necessity beyond the world of its natural humanism, beyond the philosophies and communal perceptions that called the genre into being, beyond the alliance of signifier and signified, in a word-anxious history, a new state of mythlessness, hungering for story. So much understood, we might still then go forward. The novel as we know it being dead, it must come alive as something else: a new mode of narrative, post-realist, post-humanist, and – if modernism means the redemption of a formless modern world through the realization of significant form – post-modernist. A new and saving post-fiction, metafiction or surfiction is our logical art, and so we pass beyond apocalypse.

The other view has greater historical modesty, but a strong aesthetic claim. It urges that there has been no death of the novel: rather a pluralization of its means, an opening out of its stylistic possibilities, an enriched funding of its presence, a latter-day promiscuity of its forms. The novel has not lost its power to name, record and engage moral passions; the man-

17

ners of realism are by no means exhausted, though nowadays they are likely to be deeply infiltrated with the complex, questioning deposits of modernism. The classic enquiry of fiction into the human person, and his relations with society and history, has not gone; and the so-called death of the subject which causes our despair and our displacement is not necessarily total, for the fictional imagination possesses the means by which it might be recovered against the witness of other modes of knowing, other scientific theories. The novel's moral humanism is by no means defeated, therefore, though it remains, as indeed it always was, provisional; the novel persists, as Saul Bellow emphatically phrased it in his 1976 Nobel Prize acceptance speech, as a 'sort of latter-day lean-to, a hovel in which the spirit takes shelter'. It may deal with a dark modern history, but its subject is not necessarily the death of the self or the collapse of the referential. Thus, in that speech, Bellow explicitly attacks the French *nouveau roman*, and above all Alain Robbe-Grillet's view of the death of the novel of characters ('The novel of characters belongs entirely in the past. It describes a period: that which marked the apogee of the individual'). Indeed, Bellow goes on to suggest, the novel's power to depict the complexity of the individual was never more necessary, since in our time so many processes and so many theories are arrayed against it.

In contemporary fiction, both of these views have been both active and creatively productive. Indeed, in many of our best novels and novelists we may see a curious, debating marriage between their claims (in 'magical realism', in the oscillations of novelists between faction and extreme fictiveness, in much contemporary fantasy and grotesquerie, in the novels of writers as various as Vladimir Nabokov, Iris Murdoch, Peter Handke and John Fowles). Yet the contention is crucial, because it articulates our present uncertainties about the naming status of the word and the text, and about the kind of stylistic deliverance our time might elicit from a writer who is both aesthetically and historically alert. Good and serious reasons underlie our art of vacancies and abstractions, of tragic

18

depersonalizations and deconstructed selves, of stories that fail to yield story, myths that prove mythless, our plots of indeterminacy, chance and reflexive self-consciousness. Real changes in the arts are, after all, significant parallels to fundamental changes in other structures in the world and in the political, intellectual and linguistic modes by which we interpret them; to be more than an innocent record of experience, art must always test itself stylistically. The making of the arts involves, in its best practitioners, a deep historical realization; it is to the presence of such a historical realization that we refer when we talk of style, hoping to mean not simply an individual personal signature but a radical intervention into the history and culture of the age. And it is thus possible to read in much of this modern writing, where the signifier floats free of the signified, a historical state of affairs – a state of affairs for which structuralism and post-structuralism have provided a post-Marxist and post-Freudian end-of-the-century philosophy.

Yet, as Bellow argues, the novel as a mode of knowing is capable of its own kind of witness, and possesses an inward capacity to struggle against inevitablist theories. The writer privileges imaginative writing, as he must; his path outruns criticism and transgresses theory, however much, as a thinking citizen of his time, he must absorb its meanings. One of the things we value in art and writing, without quite knowing it, is a historical alertness; it is one of the tasks of the critic to attempt to determine which stylistic phenomena seem in this sense 'authentic'. One reason that I have chosen to write about Saul Bellow, in the context of this series, is that he seems to me to stand in the middle of the consequent tensions. It has been his experience to enjoy this kind of stylistic authorization in the 1950s and early 1960s, when his mode of Jewish-American fiction seemed to represent an essential path onward, formally and morally, from modernism; and then, in the later 1960s and 1970s, to see this substantially challenged, as the direction of contemporary fictional enquiry seemed to turn – a turn which, in fact, his work seems to me to register and respond to. I want to explore his changing stylistic manners as these develop

19

through his so far nine novels and novellas: his resilience, his attentiveness to style and history, his battle with the offered logics and the age's dominant – to use a Bellovian phrase – reality-instructors. For he seems to me a figure still central to contemporary fiction, standing at the centre of changes and movements which are, at the beginning of the 1980s, as uncertain and fluid as ever they were: a writer modernly aware and internationally conscious, whose career exemplifies many of our time's sharpest artistic questions and anxieties.

*

In 1976, the Bicentennial year, Saul Bellow – the Jewish-American novelist who was in fact born of Russian-Jewish immigrants in Lachine, Quebec, Canada, and who grew up in the Montreal ghetto until at the age of 9 his family moved to his warmly adopted city of Chicago – was awarded the Nobel Prize for Literature. He won it at the age of 61, by which date he had behind him a record of seven major novels, one novella, a good number of short stories, several plays and essays, written over thirty-five years, and the reputation in many quarters of being the leading American novelist of the post-war generation. The award was doubtless intended to recognize the extent to which American fiction had, especially over the post-war period, come to dominate the international development of the novel as a genre. Also, given the spirit of the prize, it meant to recognize that Bellow, in a time when the humanistic development of the novel form had come under a severe questioning, was ready to express and speak for its humanistic purposes. Previous American novelists to win the prize had included Sinclair Lewis, William Faulkner, Ernest Hemingway and John Steinbeck, and in all four the award had been preceded by a movement in their work toward a more humanist intention.

Indeed to glance at the previous winners is to be reminded that the Nobel Prize has never been an easy one to have and to hold, especially if the author is American – part of a cultural system where the prize is tight-bonded to the complex economic operations of the culture-market, in which celebrity is both functional and self-destructive, and in which (as Bellow indi-

20

cates wryly in *Humboldt's Gift*) capitalism gives writers money for dark comical reasons of its own. The first American holder was Sinclair Lewis, who won it in 1930, after some assiduous canvassing. 'This is fatal. I cannot live up to it', he is reported to have said on hearing of the award. 'I am past fifty now; there is probably not much more in the tank', said William Faulkner in 1950, on hearing of his. 'I feel that what remains after thirty years of work is not worth carrying from Mississippi to Sweden, just as I feel that what remains does not deserve to expend the prize on himself.' 'I should have had the damn thing long ago', Hemingway complained on winning in 1954, 'I'm thinking of telling them to shove it.' He also said, 'no son of a bitch that ever won the Nobel Prize ever wrote anything worth reading afterwards.' 'This would be good if I were ready to die or if I were material for a priesthood', Steinbeck wrote in a letter when he won in 1962. And in another: 'The last book of Faulkner's was written long ago. Hemingway went into a kind of hysterical haze. Red Lewis just collapsed into alcoholism and angers. It has in effect amounted to an epitaph.' Again and again, the prize has come to seem a retrospective challenge to a whole career, a moment of institutionalization where the writer attains extreme fame but loses all flexibility and relevance.[1]

Similarly the prize speeches have always appeared a dangerous hurdle. These writers had all been part of that extraordinary inter-war achievement which had reconciled an American naturalism with a cosmopolitan modernism, and given American fiction a world reputation and a remarkably modern form. All had been associated with negation or nihilism: Lewis with a critical satire of American life on Main Street, Faulkner with an art of historical crisis and collapse, Hemingway with the existential reductionism of the 'lost generation', Steinbeck with a political dissent from dark Depression America. Yet the prize coincided with their voicing of a later-life affirmation. Faulkner's speech famously declared that he declined 'to accept the end of man'. 'A writer should write what he has to say and not speak it', said Hemingway, choosing to send his speech to

Stockholm rather than attend – to discover to his irritation that only his later work was selected out for praise, the earlier being dismissed as 'brutal, cynical, and callous'. Affirmation, then, is part of the Nobel spirit; hence, not surprisingly, the prize has been linked more with the transcendentalist rather than the modernist-nihilist face of American fiction.

Bellow was the first of the post-war American generation to be honoured, but his work does appear to lie in the same affirmative tradition, even if at a more meditative end of it. Many of Bellow's critics have read him in that way, and his own Stockholm speech was indeed affirmatively humanistic in spirit. At the same time a typical note of sceptical resilience surrounded his comments: he told one reporter that 'even though I have been at it for nearly four decades, I have always felt myself, as a writer, to be an apprentice or a journeyman', explained to another that he was 'a bit embarrassed by the Nobel Prize because I haven't got my teeth into things yet' and he also remarked,

> I feel it is time to write about people who make a more spirited resistance to the forces of our time. . . . I am not saying that, as a novelist, I have suddenly become super-ambitious. Not at all. What I am saying is that I think it is time for me to move on.[2]

That 'spirited resistance', the meditative theme of his recent novels, including the post-prize *The Dean's December* (1982), is the haunting concern of his speech, about the role of the artist in an age of crisis, though also of misleading crisis-interpretation. Bellow's novels are haunted by a large, apocalyptic gloom in the face of modern affairs, modern violence and the modern mind. But the problem faced by the artist is to discover what means he has in his art to penetrate both into and beyond them. As he puts it in the speech:

> The unending cycle of crises that began with the First World War has formed a kind of person, one who has lived through terrible, strange things, and in whom there is an observable

shrinkage of prejudices, a casting off of disappointing ideologies, an ability to live with many kinds of madness, an immense desire for certain durable human goods – truth, for instance, or freedom, or wisdom.

That need for the shattered rediscovery of fundamental truths is clearly Bellow's expectation for the novel, and in these comments (as in other statements elsewhere) he has firmly presented himself as a writer urgent in pursuit of a 'broader, more flexible, fuller, more coherent, more comprehensive account of what we human beings are, who we are, and what this life is for'.[3]

Yet, as the speech implies, there can be no discounting of the 'terrible, strange things', the modern forces denying not only the self but the articulation of *any* transcendental vision of man. The languages of its expression are at risk; Bellow's heroes – usually intellectuals, often writers, and men concerned to discern what he calls in *The Victim* 'the queerness of existence' – face constant victimization and defeat, and, for a writer critical of modern apocalyptics, his own work is remarkably dominated by apocalyptic views of history. It is indeed because these destructive historical pressures are so strong in Bellow's work, shaping their intuitions and their form, that his books compel us so strongly, in their form and their ideas and in their criticism of forms and ideas. Bellow's transcendental intentions – so apparent in the endings of his novels, in which some critics have seen an unearned rhetorical afflatus – *are* an essential direction of his work, and part of his philosophy of the novel's power for us; but so, equally, is his sense of, and his extraordinary power to create in fiction, the historical mire in which we live. A sense of victimization, of alien distance, of bleak historical inheritance, of some deeply rooted disaster functioning within contemporary consciousness, is the authentic Bellovian note. Recently the critics have chosen to emphasize the transcendentalist Bellow, his search for the higher intimations; but in his work those moves toward affirmation and the sense of the strangeness and promise of existence

23

always arise amid the perplexities and the paradoxes of life and death, and above all those of time and history – a history conceived increasingly as a tragic and systematic process to which the novelist owes full attention. If Bellow has attacked other novelists for their despair, their concern with the embattled self, their refusal to grant a high value to human nature, he has certainly not pursued his own enquiries into the matter by avoiding the historical condition in which we live. As he stresses in many of his novels, and especially in *The Dean's December*, we all live within the Hegelian understanding that tells us that the spirit of our own time is in us by nature, and that the hope for some pure and poetic detachment from it is impossible. It is, in fact, that endless pressure from our historical condition that keeps shaping and then re-shaping the nature of Bellow's work, giving his novels their sharp difference one from another, and making them – as in this study I shall argue that they are – a historically alert, formally changing, but ever persisting enquiry into a historically troubled age: in short, a developing *œuvre*.

*

Bellow's works, I am saying, are intensely contemporary and are certainly firmly placed amid the directions, tendencies and epistemologies that have shaped and then been amended in the novel of today. Bellow is an intellectual writer, and his sense of literary debts and derivations is serious and explicit: they are debts of great variousness. There is a clear debt to Emerson, Melville and the American Transcendentalists (Bellow refers to them often, either directly or by allusion, conspicuously, for example, in the ending of *Herzog*) and to the massed heritage of European Romanticism. There is another clear debt to Dreiser and the tradition of naturalism, deeply powerful in both its bleak and its optimistic forms in American fiction. Bellow often refers to this tradition, in both its ironizing and its vitalistic aspects (especially in *The Adventures of Augie March*), and has praised Dreiser, another Chicago novelist, for opening the American novel to the power of the unmediated, the open fact of American life, the commanding chaotic force of the Amer-

24

ican city. The debt also goes further, shaping Bellow's lasting struggle with the deterministic inheritance. His books show a deep sense of environmental intrusion, of the power of the conditioned, of life as competitive struggle chaotically releasing and suppressing energy. As a novelist he encounters an urban, mechanical, massed world – in which the self may be ironized, displaced or sapped by dominant processes and the laws of social placing, where victimization is real, and the assertion of self and the distillation of an act of will or a humanistic value is a lasting problem. Much of this naturalistic lore Bellow inherited from the 1930s, at the end of which he began to write. But what intersects with all this, and makes his work so convincing, is the deep penetration of his work by the classic stock of European modernism, especially that modernism in its more historically alert, post-romantic and humanistically defeated forms.

Bellow is thus a novelist of a very different generation from that of Lewis, Faulkner, Hemingway, Steinbeck or James T. Farrell, all of whom might in different ways be associated with the centralizing of the American novel as a major twentieth-century form of expression. He is a novelist writing beyond the end of American pastoral; his works belong to a new order of American and world history.

His social and ethnic origins, as a child of Russian-Jewish immigrants, connected him readily with the neo-modernist Jewish writing of the 1920s and 1930s, from Babel to Singer, from Bruno Schultz to Kafka. Politically active in the Depression, he none the less started to write in the mood of abeyance to dialectical politics that came with the Second World War; his first story, 'Two Morning Monologues', appeared (in the summer of 1941) in *Partisan Review* – that New York centred, predominantly Jewish, ex-Marxist intellectual journal moving at this date from thirties Trotskyism toward an increased commitment to the spirit of literary modernism, with its bleaker view of man in history. His earliest fictional publication thus immediately precedes the Japanese attack on Pearl Harbor which plunged America into the Second World War, collapsed the thirties political spectrum and allied Americans with the bleakness and bloodiness of modern world history. It was a history that disoriented the liberal progressive expectations of the American left, challenged naturalism as a language of political attention, and raised the question of art's response to a totalitarian and genocidal world. Bellow's response was to write about an America newly exposed to history, affected by the desperations of existentialism and absurdism, war-pained, urban, materialist, *Angst*-ridden, troubled with global responsibility, struggling to distil meaning and morality from the chaos of utopian and progressive thought.

All this was very apparent in *Dangling Man*, Bellow's first full-length novel, which appeared in 1944, as the war moved to an end – an extraordinary book which displays clear debts to a modern European writing of romantic disorientation and historical enclosure that comes from Dostoevsky, Conrad, Sartre and Camus. It is not hard to draw links between his and Dostoevsky's spiritually agonized heroes – caught in the fragmentations of a culture collapsing into urban strangeness, political disorder and waning faith which struggles with existential desire; nor between his world and Conrad's, where civilization is a thin veneer overlying anarchy, calling forth 'absurd' existential affirmations; nor between his imaginings and Kafka's, where the self moves solipsistically through an onerously powerful yet incomprehensible historical world. Yet it is as if this was a tradition which Bellow felt he had the power to qualify and amend, to recall toward humanism; and here his Jewish sources are deeply relevant, constituting another force that 'Europeanizes' his fiction.

Perhaps Isaac Bashevis Singer rather than Kafka – Bellow translated Singer's story 'Gimpel the Fool' – better suggests this origin, with his classic images of suffering and victimization irradiated with transcendental and mystical hopes; the recovering victim and the 'suffering joker' are part of the essential stuff of Bellow's writing, but so is that sense of human bonding which allows him to struggle toward a latter-day humanism and a new civility. Indeed it was that new civility, accommodating the experience of persecution and the path of survival, that made Bellow seem so central a figure in the post-war world, a world post-holocaust and post-atomic, urban and material, where progressive naturalism and innocent liberalism no longer spoke recognizably to experience.

Bellow thus went on to become a primary voice of a time when the Jewish-American writer, urban, historically alert, concerned to distil a morality and a possible humanism from a bland, material, encroaching reality in which all substantial meanings seemed hidden, moved to the centre of American writing. For now, as Leslie Fiedler noted, the Jewish hero, practised in suffering and survival, persecution and accommodation, became the type of modern man, 'the metropolitan at home, though expert in the indignities, rather than the amenities, of urban life'.[4] It was an anxious new writing, of mythic inclinations, concerned to measure the large questions of human nature against the material and conformist face of an American life which offered individualist rewards yet base compromises; in Bellow, Bernard Malamud, Delmore Schwartz, Philip Roth and others, the image of disoriented man, the parvenu in the culture, the stranger in the city, the wanderer displaced between origins and the present, offering to substantiate the culture if that culture will show its humane substance, became a central theme for the American fiction of a troubled age.

Bellow, like many of these others, drew his strength from an irritable energy of dissent, and an artistically vigorous view of Jewish metaphysical perception, which attempted to pursue connectedness and moral responsibility in a world that insisted either on bland incorporation into society or else self-privatization, a 'hoarding of spiritual valuables', as Bellow would put it (NT, p. 56). He was to prove most Jewish in his hunger to find a ceremonial of life in a darkened world, to discover some oblique act of human faith. 'The world comes after you . . .', Joseph, the disoriented, hermetic, intellectual protagonist of Dangling Man, moving in spirit away from coercive society, reflects. 'Whatever you do you cannot dismiss it.' But the new humanism was hard to forge, being riddled with doubts and fears – aware of the disjunctive implications of modern experience and modernist writing, conscious of the dark threats of modern totalitarian force, of the justice of apocalyptic imaginings and of the troubled warnings of Freud and others about the imbalance of civilization and desire.

Bellow thus developed as a writer in a period when a distinct stylistic and aesthetic climate, which was also a political climate, was forming. It was a period of revived liberalism, invigorated by the reaction against totalitarianism that arose with the battle against and then the defeat of Nazism, and then with the new cold war struggle of the superpowers. The politics and aesthetics of liberalism were an important version of recovered pluralism and democracy; yet at the same time the post-war social order, with its materialism, its pressure toward conformity, its move toward mass society, threatened the liberal self. The reaction against totalitarian models shaped aesthetic and formal choices; both the lore of modernism and that of naturalism, especially in its thirties form as politico-social realism, came under question. The 1950s seemed hungry for a post-political politics, a post-ideological ideology; in this process literature and cultural concern became the foci of intellectual activity. Modern literature, with its sense of irony, scruple and moral ambiguity, with its bleak report on modern *Angst* and exposure, replaced more ideological texts, especially those of 1930s Marxism, the God that had failed. In the new mood of political abeyance, where there was a strong concern for the rediscovery of a moral humanism that might redeem suffering and destruction, literature became a mode of anxious moral and metaphysical exploration.

It was the Jewish writers, with their sense of traditional alienation and exile, their profoundly relevant witness to the recent holocaust, their awareness of the inadequacies of an older liberalism that could not cope with what Reinhold Niebuhr called 'the ultimately religious problem of the evil in man', who concentrated the spirit of the necessary imagination. Lionel Trilling would call this 'the liberal imagination', whose natural centre lies in the novel, the testing place where the ideal is perpetually forced to mediate with the contingent and the real, where ideology meets 'the hum and buzz of culture', where history and individual are compelled into encounter.[5]

Bellow's fiction, as it developed from the tight form of *Dangling Man* (1944) and *The Victim* (1947) into the looser and more picaresque structures of *The Adventures of Augie March* (1953) and *Henderson the Rain King* (1959), thus seemed to gesture toward a revival of the liberal novel – a form that has had a strained history in our modern and modernist century. The liberal novel is, I take it, the novel of Whiggish history, where there is some community of need between self and society, where individuals may reach out into the world of exterior relationships for reality, civility and maturity, where the possibility of moral enlargement and discovery resides. It is thus attentive to history in both individual and community, finds both equally real, and grants to both a logical chronology of growth. Bellow's novels have certainly moved toward the salvaging of a liberal form. They are hero-centred to a degree unusual in modern fiction; the hero often gives his name to the novel. He is always a man and often a Jew, and often a writer or intellectual; he is anxious about 'self', concerned with exploring its inward claim, and about 'mind', which may be our salvation or the real source of our suffering. At the same time he is driven by an irritable desire to recognize his relation with others, with society as such, with the felt texture of common existence, with nature and the universe. Around such battles certain prime reminders occur: man is mortal, and death must be weighed; man is biologically in process, part of nature, and must find his measure in it; man is consciousness, and consciousness is indeed in history; man is real, but so is the world in its historical evolution, and the two substantialities evade understandable relation. So we are drawn toward thoughts of extreme alienation, urgent romantic selfhood, apocalyptic awareness, while at the same time we know ourselves to be in a post-romantic universe, Lenin's age of wars and revolutions, where our conditioning is inescapable. Social and historical existence may thus contend with mythical or metaphysical existence, but neither can finally outweigh the other, and the effort must be toward reconciliation – an end displayed in Bellow's own fictional endings, which frequently take the form of some complex contractual renewal between the self and the world, though, despite critical suspicion of them, these endings are less some rhetorical resolution than a suspended anxiety, often returned to in the next novel.

Bellow's books could thus be said to stand at the centre of contemporary enquiry into the possibilities of the novel – an enquiry inherited from those writers of the turn of the century who made naïve realism problematic. For the late Henry James, the novel was driven back symbolistically on to itself, becoming an exploration into the relationship between the perceptions of consciousness and the materiality of the exterior world; in Dreiser's fiction, that materiality becomes a process, a set of systems far larger than the consciousnesses they conditioned, and making them into a facet of things. For the contemporary writer, this space – between what Bellow calls in *Humboldt's Gift* the 'it' and the 'we' – has been a fundamental area of search. In Bellow's novels, consciousness and history struggle at odds, in a world where, as Joseph notes in *Dangling Man*, the old metaphysical stage of good and evil has been reset, and 'under this revision, we have, instead, only history to answer to' (*DM*, p. 73). Yet history may indeed point to excrescence or emptiness, or else to a Byzantine therapeutic self-celebration, a fashionable contemporaneity unaware of its own illusions and decadences. On the one hand there is a lack of cosmic fit between individual and the social mass, the endless proliferation of technologies, systems and abstract social relations; on the other there is the hidden administration of power, truth, 'reality' which makes that inner life an aspect of the process from which it seeks to separate itself. Thus there is alienation as a false romantic solipsism, and there is determination as a false acquiescence; the problem of Bellow's heroes, and of Bellow's novels, is to discover the spaces and the

30

places of that which is both unconditioned and humanly alert and present.

It is indeed because Bellow's novels have in them an intense historical presence that they have survived so vigorously over the four decades of his writing. For many of Bellow's contemporaries, the strain of mastering contemporary American experience has not been easy to face. The Jewish-American novel of the 1940s and 1950s was displaced, in the 1960s, by a novel of historical extremism (*Catch-22*, *Slaughterhouse-Five*) or historical senselessness (*V.*). Indeed, as Morris Dickstein puts it in his *Gates of Eden* (1977), 'one of those deep-seated shifts of sensibility that alters the whole moral terrain' occurred, as a new provisionalist radicalism challenged the post-war 'new liberal' synthesis.[6] The moral containments of fifties fiction gave way to new aesthetics of black humour, counter-cultural provisionality, irrationalism and outrage; the new postmodernist text appeared, lexically complex but moving toward indeterminacy of meaning. The non-fiction novel, founded on the conviction that the extremist realities of 1960s America was itself an absurd fiction, linked with the new fictionality. On the writers of the 1940s and 1950s, the impact was clear. J. D. Salinger, whose fragile moral redemptions had seemed an essential metaphysics of possibility, followed his own Glass family into an elected, aesthetic silence. Norman Mailer turned from a formalized naturalism to a fiction of historical self-immersion, offering himself up as a secret agent of the *Zeitgeist*, a risk-taking performer active and participant in the cannibalism of contemporary sensibility. Bernard Malamud's later fiction displayed the strain of applying formal artistic expectations to the unnerving new landscape of modern politicized consciousness; Philip Roth moved from the Jamesian moral management of his early books into the free-form confessional of his later ones.

As for the balance and nature of Bellow's work, that too changed. In the 1950s he had explored the expansive epic, testing out whether man can set himself free in history. By the 1960s that enquiry had tightened again, into the complex

31

structural form of *Herzog* (1964), where historical presence becomes a form of madness, and the bleak irony of *Mr Sammler's Planet* (1970), which now looks less a bitter assault on the new radicalism than the beginning of a new kind of enquiry into the elements of evil secreted in our modern history, and in modern America, in an age marked by post-cultural energy, a new rootless barbarism in which possibility and monstrosity contend for the soul. Bellow's books have grown not easier but harder to read. They have become in some ways more meditative, philosophical, transcendental. So Nathan A. Scott rightly says that we should not see them as some form of latter-day naturalism, but as works where the phenomenology of selfhood is at stake, so that they turn on essential moments when the hero, 'transcending the immediate pressures of his environment and the limiting conditions of his social matrix, asks himself some fundamental question about the nature of his own humanity' — a question increasingly answered, Scott suggests, by a falling into peace, a submission to the multi-layered mystery of existence.[7] Bellow's lasting concern with questions of the nature of our human contract, our eternality, the worth of our existence on this stony and historically troubled planet, has extended and grown more complex; but so, equally, has his concern with the definition of our late age, the darkening life of our century, the engulfing mechanisms of power and mass, the anxious performance of a consciousness ever more drawn toward excess and extremity.

Bellow is not, in the fashionable sense of the term, a 'post-modern' or even an 'experimental' novelist. He does not question reflexively his own fictionality, or adopt the nihilist stoicism of black humour. His books still grant the dominant materiality of the outer world, which is process, system and power; and they continue to explore consciousness and mind in struggle with that power, as they hunt to find a significant human meaning, an inward presence and a sense of personal immediacy, and an outward awareness of the nature of the cosmic world. Consciousness and history still struggle at odds, but in an ever-compelled and ever-changing intimacy. His books have, indeed, largely changed by circling their own known subjects, intensifying the elements, deepening the enquiry. Bellow's perception of the nature, the substance and the pressure of the historical world has moved increasingly toward a definition of a new, post-cultural America, most clearly manifest in his own home city of Chicago, that 'cultureless city pervaded nonetheless by Mind', as its life has changed, accumulated and massed; as its old localities and ways of life fall under the hands of the new developers, as crime and terror haunt its inner city and the *inner* inner city of its inhabitants, as the doors are triple-locked and bourgeois life goes on under siege in some strange modern compact with a new barbarism, it becomes a central image of what the mind and the novel alike must come to terms with. His perception of the world of consciousness has also grown more intense and avid for right feeling, as it finds itself bereft yet busy, having nowhere else but history from which to draw versions of reality in its endless quest for awareness and fulfilment.

A novelist who registers the enormous pressure of modern life, and also the peculiar sense of existence, on a scale rare in fiction, Bellow has thus reacted with a considerable formal flexibility and variousness. Coming into being over four transforming decades of American life, his books have registered them with a vital historical *and* aesthetic attention, taking the novel form as *the* necessary mode of mediation between the world of process and the world of consciousness. A critic of apocalyptics, Bellow has grown more apocalyptic; a doubter of concepts, he has grown more conceptual and abstract, though searching always for those moments of immediacy and humanity when the soul feels its presence and its need to value existence. A voice of moral liberalism, he has grown more conservative, in a large sense, become a writer who explores the contrast between a culturally coherent past and a post-cultural present. A novelist who defends the novel's humanism, he has shown us, more than most novelists, the powers that point toward a post-humanist world, and hence challenge the novel's capacities to explore it. His books, especially his most recent, portraits of writers making the crucial attempt, show both the challenge and the indeterminacy of the solutions; in a sense, it is their indeterminacy that makes every new Bellow novel possible. Bellow not only has been, but remains, one of the most essential American writers of his age; and it is both the flexibility and the serious consistency of his enterprise I want to examine in this study.

2

THE FORTIES NOVELS:
'DANGLING MAN' AND 'THE VICTIM'

He asked himself a question I still would like answered,
namely, 'How should a good man live, what ought he to do?'
(*Dangling Man*)

In a number of interviews, Bellow has put himself at a considerable distance from his first two novels, *Dangling Man* (1944) and *The Victim* (1947), presenting them as the product of a timid and mandarin self hobbled with formality and borrowed sensibility.[8] Writers frequently make such withdrawals; and it is a sign of Bellow's wide and varied repertoire as a novelist that he should do so. Yet these two books are remarkable novels of the forties; concentrating the change that was coming over American fiction in that decade, they also display the intellectual and emotional foundations of all Bellow's subsequent writing, and the cosmopolitan intellectual sources from which it springs. Both are somewhat of a kind, melancholic and pure in form (though hardly, as Bellow has it, 'Flaubertian'); they lack the spaciousness and ebullience of his later works. But in their tightness and enclosure they are deeply appropriate to the season in which they appeared – the wartime and post-war period when an agonized existentialism and a sense of human absurdity seeking outward for recovery or commitment had become a dominant intellectual language, when feelings of historical and social victimization were strong. Such themes link the books to earlier Jewish-American fiction, a lineage developing from the 1890s, and perhaps most to books like Abraham Cahan's *The Rise of David Levinsky* (1917) and Henry Roth's *Call It Sleep* (1934), where immigrant naturalism crosses with experimental modernism. But there were other obvious sources: what is notable about the books is their cosmopolitanism, their outreach toward modern European fiction.

Especially there is a debt to European modernism in its bleaker and more historically painful forms: to those tales of the underground man and the double, the man without qualities and the man of no feeling, the lonely witness in the city and the post-romantic solipsist in the assailing landscape, which had explored the psychology and fictional methodology of modern estrangement. In particular *Dangling Man* is inconceivable without Babel, Kafka and Sartre. It is a book about an intelligent, sceptical, romantic figure in a post-romantic world, written in the manner of absurdist diary literature, which takes Joseph, the self-recording protagonist, dangling between work and military induction, politics and inner need, a marginal man with 'in a word, no character', into Kafkaesque enclosure and solitude. His condition is explicitly 'existential' – he is not able to find essence in existence – and Sartre's novel *La Nausée* (1938) clearly echoes in it as its agent seeks to bring nature and good faith back to both himself and the outward world by discovering an adequate act of commitment, self-surrender making for self-discovery. The book has rightly been seen as one of the best American war novels, far as it is from any battlefield; in fact it captures not only the wartime atmosphere but the haunting crisis about political bad faith that developed during the years of cold war, rising materialism and what Daniel Bell called 'the end of ideology'. It can now be read as a work of curious ambiguity, simultaneously asserting and denying 'alienation' – the 'fool's plea' Joseph is struggling with throughout the novel (p. 113). But that doubleness was then to characterize most of Bellow's novels, which move between a battle for social and historical engagement and a quest for the eternal signals of humanity.

Dangling Man is set in 1942 in the denatured city – Bellow's adopted home town, Chicago – as its central figure resigns his job in expectation of his much-resented induction into the army and waits in one room, supported by his wife, in a condition of irritable suffering – a condition he will share with many of Bellow's later heroes. He lives in a time of too much history and no politics, of too much mass and no being; he has been a Marxist during the 1930s, a devotee, as he says, of *le genre humain*, and he knows we have history to answer to. But political urgency and passion no longer serves, and the desire to coerce history has left him. He has also been in the past a man in whom wonder has been more important than judgement, devoted to

> speculation on men, drugged and clear, jealous, ambitious, good, tempted, curious, each in his own time and with his customs and motives, and bearing the imprint of strangeness in the world. In a sense, everything is good because it exists. Or, good or not good, it exists, it is ineffable, and, for that reason, marvellous. (p. 24)

Joseph has thus possessed a sharpened and open sense of existence, but he also has the desire to know himself, 'to know what we are and what we are for, to know our purpose, to seek grace' (p. 128). All this may be seen as the Bellovian map of desire, the world in tension in his fictions; the problem in this book, as in so many of Bellow's novels, is what happens when the sense of existence and the sense of self come into conflict.

Joseph is a clerkly intelligent man of humanist aspirations, struggling between outward history and inner freedom and finding that there are no adequate laws for their connection – that essential anxiety of contemporary fiction. The book starts off with his assertion of the need of the self to be articulate: 'There was a time when people were in the habit of addressing themselves frequently and felt no shame at making a record of their inward transactions' (p. 7). But now the discourse is weakened and shame exists. Joseph begins to discover why: inward transactions are dependent on outward transactions, and it is these that the world has progressively suppressed in its modern order and state of being. Thus the book is conspicuously dominated by a passage from a text of fundamental romantic expectation, Goethe's *Poetry and Life*:

All comfort in life is based upon a regular occurrence of external phenomena. The changes of day and night, of the seasons, of flowers and fruits, and all other recurring pleasures that come to us, that we may and should enjoy them – these are the mainsprings of our earthly life. The more open we are to these enjoyments, the happier we are; but if these changing phenomena unfold themselves and we take no interest in them, if we are insensitive to such fair solicitations, then comes on the sorest evil, the heaviest disease – we regard life as a loathsome burden. (p. 15)

But it is this romantic marriage of the life within us and abroad that the modern urban world, with history to answer to, denies, generating Joseph's mounting enclosure, his experience of life as 'loathsome burden'.

Part of the cause of that burden is the exclusion of romantic possibility in the naturalist modern city, the environmentalist power that seems to contain no particle of what has spoken in men's favour:

There could be no doubt that these billboards, streets, tracks, houses, ugly and blind, were related to interior life. And yet, I told myself, there had to be a doubt. There were human lives organized around these ways and houses, and that they, the houses, say, were the analogue, that what men created they also were, through some transcendental means, I could not bring myself to concede. There must be a difference, a quality that eluded me, somehow, a difference between things and persons and even between acts and persons. Otherwise the people who lived here were actually a reflection of the things they lived among. (p. 20)

Here is Bellow's essential theme. Joseph's search is to find a world of spirit which contains transcendental reflections of nobility; like all Bellow's heroes, he seeks to 'keep a measure of cleanliness and freedom' in spite of 'the calamity, the lies and moral buggery, the odium, the detritus of wrong and sorrow dropped on every human heart'. He finds only those who are 'dispersed into separate corners, incommunicado', an 'inner

38

climate of darkness', which locks him into the prison of his chosen freedom, the realm of self-government outside the social life and in his private room, where 'the perspectives end in the walls'. Imprisoned between romantic solipsism and a gross determinism, seeking the ideal freedom, 'one that unlocks the imprisoning self', he confronts inner adversaries, beginning to discover 'the ephemeral agreements by which we live and pace ourselves'. Finally, in a collusion of nature, he is 'done', ready for surrender; he offers himself to the army as 'available at any time'. Aware of the treachery of familiar objects of common sense, he submits to compulsory civility: the book ends on his final cry of self-abnegation:

> I am no longer to be held accountable for myself: I am grateful for that. I am in other hands, relieved of self-determination, freedom cancelled.
> Hurray for regular hours!
> And for supervision of the spirit!
> Long live regimentation! (p. 159)

The book thus ends on an ambiguity of tone that has tested the critics: Joseph's cry is a testament of loss, a testament of gain, an acquiescence in the defeat of the solitary free spirit in its solipsism, but an embrace of historical attachment, enforced community, the 'uniform of the times'. In that ambiguity it becomes an existentially modern novel, a turn against the separate peace of Hemingway's fiction. It seems a bleak naturalist tale of defeat by the contingent modern city, where 'great pressure is brought to bear to make us undervalue ourselves', promoting a sense of being's unnecessariness, the waning of the self; it also expresses itself as a very Jewish novel, looking for the recovered community in such a world. Joseph is involved with others 'because whether I liked it or not, they were my generation, my society, my world. We were figures in the same plot, eternally together. I was aware, also, that their existence, just as it was, made mine possible' (p. 20). Joseph's acceptance of the system in its bureaucracy and violent inadequacy is a dark paradox that would resound through much American writing of the post-war period; it resembles the compromise between broken liberalism and modern force that Norman Mailer explores in that other key war novel, *The Naked and the Dead* (1948). And what distinguishes Bellow's treatment is already his transforming vein of Jewish metaphysical rhetoric, so much concerned with what Joseph calls *le genre humain*, which constitutes his final cause and validates both his suffering and his self-abasement; his limited acceptance of the inadequate world is the characteristic Bellovian note.

*

This is the theme extended in Bellow's next, fuller novel *The Victim*, another work set among the determining pressures in a naturalistic, oppressive New York, and telling another tale of social responsibility discovered and enforced in a world where the task of self-definition seems thrown wholly upon the individual. Now, however, the meaning of the novel is greater than that of the experience of the central figure; Bellow gives up first-person diary form for third-person narrative, telling of a few days in the life of Asa Leventhal, a young Jewish professional man moving gradually from failure to success in magazine publishing. Leventhal has 'accidentally' caused a Gentile acquaintance, Kirby Allbee (the name has obvious significance), to lose his job, and throughout the larger part of the book Leventhal is pursued by the repulsive Allbee and forced to inspect the nature of the 'accidental' and to determine the degree and nature of his responsibility for the other. It seems, in a naturalist world, that there is none. 'On some nights New York is as hot as Bangkok', the book begins; the city, its heat, the crowds and the general abrasiveness of urban existence dominate; life is a struggle not only with other persons but with impersonal forces – like the subway doors closing on Leventhal as he enters the train as the story begins – and obstructive barriers – like the ferry he must take to Staten Island when he goes to see his brother's family. The great circle of humanity whirls in a system of indifference and hostility; most of Leventhal's encounters are in fact with crowds, on the ferry, in the subway, the street, the cafeterias and office blocks.

40

Most are abrasive: love slides and families disintegrate; his brother leaves wife and children, Leventhal's marriage is flawed by memories of his wife's previous lover, and for much of the action she is away, leaving Leventhal without love's support. The city is thus a melting pot, a dense agglomeration of misery and competition, a place of tenuous relationships, run by mysterious blacklists and arbitrary decisions. And Leventhal is a lonely man in the agglomerate, a man for whom the presence of so many other people is a permanent threat, a small survivor of petty bourgeois struggles who has 'got away with it' but always fears he will fall again. This feeling of insecurity creates the novel's mood of containment and tension, its world in which every man feels he is a victim, in which some must go to the wall and the individual's task is to make sure that it is not he. As Allbee says:

> We don't choose much. We don't choose to be born, for example, and unless we commit suicide we don't choose the time to die, either. But having a few choices in between makes you seem less of an accident to yourself. It makes you feel your life is necessary. The world's a crowded place, damned if it isn't. . . . Do you want anything? . . . There are a hundred million others who want that very same thing. I don't care whether it's a sandwich or a seat in the subway or what. . . . Who wants all these people to be here, especially for ever? (p. 159)

Life is thus a struggle of chances, in which, ironically enough, it is Allbee's task to educate Leventhal in the law of responsibility, for it is he who feels the sensibility of the victim. For this is a world in which no equable mean of life exists; there is no clear system of class or hierarchy, and no promises have been made in advance, so that all races suspect persecution; no moral scale seems to fit all cases, and any personal order created by the individual seems constantly challenged and threatened. As Allbee feels there is a Jewish 'set-up', so Leventhal feels there is a blacklist against all Jews; a suppressed racial anger and a sense of general injustice rages in the book. It is this

41

that generates Leventhal's irritability, the effective cause of Allbee's dismissal from his job. Anti-semitism is a crucial theme of the novel; it is present not only in Allbee, who sees himself displaced from his rightful status in American society, his WASP entitlement ('The world's changed hands', he says. 'I'm like the Indian who sees a train running over the prairie where the buffalo used to roam' (p. 181)), but in Leventhal himself. Unlike Joseph, who becomes 'absurd' in his refusal to see himself as conditioned, like others, Leventhal sees himself as conditioned only, and acquires the opposed mode of absurdity, a lasting sense of insecurity that intrudes into all his relations with others. He lives in a world and a psyche conditioned by the fear of falling and failing; Allbee constitutes the main form of danger because he has no sense that either success or failure may be 'deserved', but that they are the result of the wilful persecutions of others or of random good or ill luck.

An essential theme of *The Victim* is the relation between the accidental and the connected, the contingent and the necessary. It is this theme that is brought home to us by the novel's great imaginative invention, of the inescapable stranger: Allbee rises up before Leventhal out of the anonymous crowd to say *You!*, asserts that the two of them are not disconnected but connected, and attempts to impose on Leventhal the meaning and responsibility involved in that connection, asking him, in effect, for a new view of the world. The critics have rightly read strong traces of Dostoevsky in this, and drawn particular parallels between the book and Dostoevsky's novellas *The Eternal Husband* and *The Double*, where the theme of the crucial double appears, generating not just psychic mirrorings but patterns of suffering and victimization. Allbee is the ostensible victim who anti-semitically victimizes Leventhal. He assaults not only his emotional tightness and his inward sense of a 'fault' but also his principles of moral order: his firm conviction of right and wrong, his insecure conviction that the world rewards those who deserve and pushes down those who do not, who may include himself, his instinct to blame others and himself, his suspicion and his separatism, his touchy

42

conviction *of* persecution. At the same time Allbee needs someone to accuse of his misfortune in order not to blame *himself*; but his idea of a random fall into the outcast state is just what Leventhal fears most.

The concerns of *The Victim* are condensed into one of the epigraphs that precede the book – a tale from *The Thousand and One Nights* of a merchant who eats a date in the desert and throws away the stone 'with force'; an Ifrit appears and threatens to kill him, because the stone has struck and killed the Ifrit's invisible son. This is a resonant fable of responsibility and the ease with which we violate the universe around us. Coleridge gave it its romantic meaning by invoking it in connection with *The Ancient Mariner*, where the mariner arbitrarily halts someone in the wedding crowd and says *You!* But Bellow's world is apparently one of deathliness rather than a living fabric; his city is, as in *Dangling Man*, a naturalist jungle, a barbarous place sliding toward the equator, stirring with energy but also unnaturally dead, filled with wild psychic activity and barrenness in which wild furies erupt.

Bellow cannot establish a direct or political social connection between Leventhal and Allbee, nor a romantic moral one: the eliciting of an adequate morality for such a world is indeed the central problem of the book. This is a world in which the accidental *is* necessary – something that Bellow emphasizes by his chronological structure in the novel. Though its logical temporal sequence would make it begin when Leventhal goes for the job interview at a magazine and loses his temper with his prospective employer over an imagined racial slight, this outburst probably helping to produce Allbee's dismissal, the book's narrative defers all this and starts on the sudden, strange encounter with an Allbee who is now down and out, menacing, unrecognizable. Likewise, emphasizing this shock, it perceives from Leventhal's point of view, but in a tone of half-detachment which emphasizes his mixed, touchy, half-absurd, comic character, his incomplete perceptions, his lasting difficulties as a man of moralities and responsibilities who cannot discriminate them, because, in this urban, competitive, racially tense, morally inchoate and shapeless society of the modern mass, such concerns are tenuous, in some real sense absurd, constantly threatened, tainted with feelings of senselessness and threatening evil.

So *The Victim* is a book about the oblique, angular bonds of moral responsibility, and in this respect is much more articulate than *Dangling Man*. But what it emphasizes is the strange psychic bonding of Leventhal and Allbee, the drama of existence intruded upon. At first Leventhal feels he has been 'singled out to be the object of some freakish, insane process' (p. 31), related to the glimpses of evil he keeps perceiving in the outward world, 'strange things, terrible things. They hung near him all the time in trembling drops, invisible, usually, or seen from a distance' (pp. 81–2). He fears the drops will fall on him. Gradually Allbee penetrates further, comes into Leventhal's apartment, evoking his disturbances and his anxieties, his sense of a troubled and doubled self, his repressed sexuality, intruding 'a depth of life in which he would be choked, lost, ended. There lay horror, evil, all he had kept himself from' (p. 224). At the same time the question of connection and responsibility grows in his conscience; he feels himself to be moving toward a 'showdown',

> a crisis that would bring an end of his resistance to something he had no right to resist. Illness, madness, and death were forcing him to confront his fault. He had used every means, and principally indifference and neglect, to avoid acknowledging it and he still did not know what it was. But that was owing to the way he had arranged not to know. He had done a great deal to make things easier for himself, toning down, softening, looking aside. But the more he tried to subdue whatever it was that he resisted, the more it raged, and the moment was coming when his strength to resist would be at an end. (p. 131)

He so comes to see in himself and others a principle of order and a principle of anarchy, something that leads to sleep and dullness and something that struggles against it: 'We were all the time taking care of ourselves, laying up, storing up, watch-

44

ing on this side and on that side, and at the same time running desperately, running as if in an egg race with the egg in a spoon' (p. 85).

The showdown thus comes not as a moral discovery but as an onrush of anarchy that destroys the 'balance' that Leventhal has guiltily constructed for himself. Allbee brings a whore into his flat and his bed; Leventhal breaks in on his 'love' and expels him; in a dream the unknown woman, already analogically connected with many other sexual hints and presences that have disturbed him, is connected with his own wife. Then Allbee returns to the flat and tries to gas himself and incidentally Leventhal; to Leventhal it seems that Allbee wants both to love and to kill. It is an onrush of horror, the end of a nightmare, in which the intermingling of identities is followed by an act of self-preservation, and so release; he can now be reborn into ordinary human life.

When we see him in the last chapter, a coda, he has been 'lucky', looks younger, and has done fairly well. Now, though, he is aware of two orders of life: one the workaday level, where success is haphazard, where people are assigned to different roles and classes, different seats in the theatre in front of the varied show of life; the other an order where 'there are more important things to be promised', a life fully lived, even though he does not live it. Allbee also reappears, seedily successful, living off an actress, 'just a passenger' on the train of life, on terms now with the first order. But the novel closes on an unanswered question from Leventhal – 'Wait a minute, what's your idea of who runs things?' he cries after Allbee (p. 238) – which refers to the incompleteness of both their solutions, and of, in a sense, the book.

The novel's larger intimations and affirmations are thus greater than its experiential story. They have been laid into the novel largely by a choric character, the old Yiddish journalist Mr Schlossberg, one of the Jewish community with which Leventhal has detached, casual dealings, a theatre critic whose affirmative perceptions of a measure of life that is extra-social and transcends both naturalism and conventional moralism

45

sound a generous Jewish hymn of human possibility through the book. 'Good acting is what is exactly human', he says early in the novel. 'And if you say I am a tough critic, you mean I have a high opinion of what is human. This is my whole idea. More than human, can you have any use for life? Less than human, you don't either' (pp. 112–13). Most actors, he says, see people as packages, most businessmen believe simply in business; neither have an idea of greatness and beauty, but

> I am as sure about greatness and beauty as you are about black and white. If a human life is a great thing to me, it *is* a great thing. Do you know better? I'm entitled as much as you. And why be measly? Do you have to be? Is somebody holding you by the neck? Have dignity, you understand me? Choose dignity. Nobody knows enough to turn it down. (p. 113)

As Leventhal comes closer to his 'showdown', begins to sense the bond with Allbee, and doubt his judgements about another crisis, that in his brother's family, this theme returns to become a speculation on the death that Leventhal is to step close to; Schlossberg remarks on the way Americans seek to evade the thought of death, failing to grant that there is a limit to every man:

> There's a limit to me. But I have to be myself in full. Which is someone who dies, isn't it? That's what I was from the beginning. I'm not three people, four people. I was born once and I will die once. You want to be two people? More than human? Maybe it's because you don't know how to be one. (p. 208)

Readers of later Bellow will see the sounding of an essential note: against the naturalism and the contingency, the protected and the workaday, there *is* an assertion to be made, an affirmation of potential within chosen limits. And if Leventhal's half-death and half-rebirth does not reach the full limits, the choric rhetoric, deeply Yiddish and metaphysical in its intonation, seeks to: against odds we may perceive a standard of a human mean, not more than human, less than human, but human exactly, which incorporates evil, threat and death without inflating or diminishing personal and collective existence.

For this reason we may read *The Victim* as a novel that steps beyond absurdism toward a recovered moralism – a form of that 'new liberal' novel that the fifties was to evolve in the work of writers like Malamud and Salinger. It expresses the massing and threat of modern urban society, and the pressure of the retreat into the self and the grotesquerie that such a self incorporates. But it also distils from the Jewish heritage a discourse of metaphysical enquiry, a language of the human predicament that seeks to press against the image of disoriented modern man in a world of urban anonymity, behavioural indifference, the totalitarian massing of social force. It is this humanism-under-pressure that now becomes Bellow's voice, the voice of a writer who, as Ihab Hassan puts it, seeks to 'convince us that reality or experience of life – call it what we will – is worth all the agonies of human existence without ever needing to be intelligible.'[9]

The Victim is Bellow's opening out into new possibilities for the novel form. The naturalist indebtedness is there: it draws on that strong American tradition which speaks for the weight and process of the material world, the power of determinants, the struggle of life in the social jungle where some arbitrarily benefit and others sink. The novel of psychological modernism leaves its mark in the figure of the inwardly pressured and absurd self. But all this is open to emendation, above all by that metaphysical sense of a human condition to be assessed which stylizes and shapes the action, heightens its meanings and effects, lyricizes experience, transfigures an apparently neo-realist perception into something vastly more theoretical, psycho-mythic, poetic, even comic. It opens the way to Bellow's vastly more expansive novels of the 1950s; but these early books, especially *The Victim*, explore the modern issues and the formal tensions and enquiries that were to remain the basis of his work, and leave them, particularly *The Victim*, among his best achievement.

3

THE FIFTIES NOVELS:
'THE ADVENTURES OF AUGIE MARCH',
'SEIZE THE DAY' AND
'HENDERSON THE RAIN KING'

> I looked in at an octopus, and the creature seemed also to look at me and press its soft head to the glass, flat, the flesh becoming pale and granular — blanched, speckled. The eyes spoke to me coldly. But even more speaking, even more cold, was the soft head with its speckles, a cosmic coldness in which I felt I was dying. The tentacles throbbed and motioned through the glass, the bubbles sped upward, and I thought, 'This is my last day. Death is giving me notice.'
> (*Henderson the Rain King*)

Bellow has often spoken of a change of style and perception that came into his work after his first two novels; it is an unmistakable feature of his fiction of the 1950s. Starting with *The Adventures of Augie March* (1953), he began to write a new kind of novel, one that broke out of the tight, European-ized, soul-searching and *Angst*-ridden form of his first books and opened into an exuberant and positive comedy. Bellow has remarked that 'modern comedy has something to do with the disintegrating outline of the worthy and humane Self, the bourgeois hero of an earlier age'; he has also seen that there is a modern comedy that ridicules the conditions of this misery, releasing pain as laughter.[10] He has remarked too on the power of the comic in the Yiddish tradition: 'Laughter and trembling are so curiously mingled that it is not easy to determine the relations of the two',[11] and this evidently has much to do with his own developing direction in comedy — one that sought to reach from the sad humour of human suffering to comic aspiration toward human grandeur, from the historical and diurnal world to the world of the transcendent and eternal. Bellow's heroes began to change; they became less victimized sufferers of insight and discovery, more positive, questing seekers after it. In the process, Bellow seemed to become a more affirmative writer, though in looking to that affirmation we must always observe the struggles and human pains out of which it grew.

As these new preoccupations shaped into matters of style and form, Bellow's novels changed. The old naturalist and existential containments did not by any means disappear, but they became a material to be contended with; his new books were texts of expansion and flow, novels of character-formation in which the heroes, especially Augie March and Henderson, became large mental travellers in quest through large social, psychic and neomythic landscapes to find the measure of their being, the nature of their human tenure. This released in Bellow a potential for mythic, fantastic and comic writing he had earlier contained, and along with it a Bellovian metaphysical vernacular, one of his larger offerings to the contemporary novel. In *The Victim* Bellow's style had already shown more suppleness, a freer motion between the hard social world and the world of thought and feeling. Now, by bringing a vital new energy and ebullience to his central characters, a new texture to his prose, Bellow was able to convert that social world into a landscape adequate to the enquiring spirit. Bellow's writing of the 1950s is thus a great opening out; in it he creates both a new form and a new kind and condition of hero. The form was that of picaresque metaphysical comedy; the heroes were self-creators, men who command large dimensions of their own fate, and move through expansive open landscapes and comic self-venturing into a growth of the spirit. The structural form expands toward contingency, toward vastly enlarged social content in *The Adventures of Augie March* (1953), toward mythic and psychological metaphor in *Henderson the Rain King* (1959), and the dominant rhetoric takes on vastly greater splendour, wit and comic self-awareness.

Bellow has since reflected that this release, coming in *The Adventures of Augie March*, was at first 'too effusive and uncritical'. 'I think I took off too many [restraints], and went too far, but I was feeling the excitement of discovery', he said in an interview. 'I had just increased my freedom, and like any emancipated plebian I abused it at once.'[12] One form of release was to admit the voice of the extravagant self-narrator; the first-person mode of *The Adventures of Augie March* immediately opens out to display him as the first of Bellow's heroes who are larger than the world in which they live. Augie may have grown up in classic Chicago, that city of naturalism, 'just plain brutal and not mitigated', and come off its mean streets. But it is clear to him that the *Studs Lonigan* containments that have limited his predecessors in fiction are not meant for him, as his expansive opening utterance makes clear:

> I am an American, Chicago born – Chicago, that sombre city – and go at things as I have taught myself, free-style, and will make the record in my own way: first to knock, first admitted; sometimes an innocent knock, sometimes a not so innocent. But a man's character is his fate, says Heraclitus, and in the end there isn't any way to disguise the nature of the knocks by acoustical work on the door or gloving the knuckles. (*AM*, p. 7)

Augie is extravagant morally, intellectually and emotionally, and in a sense he has a character by becoming a character, fictionally dense and detailed, moving in a vastly more various and established world – unlike Joseph who retires into his room and has 'in a word, no character'. As Augie feels he has all human history behind him, and wishes to embrace the quality and texture of life, to become a Columbus of the near at hand, so Bellow, with a Dickensian abundance, provides him with it. The book is Bellow's most specified and episodic, a rich, character-filled, sprawling account of 'adventures' where, in scenes of very broad texture and significance, Augie passes beyond the Machiavellians and instructors of his childhood who seek to enlist him under laws of control and limitation, and moves out into a wider kingdom of abundance where he learns not just from other men and women but from all to hand: animals, nature, books.

But, appropriately enough for a novel dealing in part with a massive, energetic, material and indeed 'sombre' Chicago during the Depression years, the battle of determinism and independence is an essential structure to the book. 'All the influences were lined up waiting for me', Augie notes. 'I was born, and there they were to form me' (p. 52). Indeed all things seem to intersect in him: the flow of history, the interaction of races and classes, intellectual theories and their 'terrible appearances' within the world. Historicism and romantic independence struggle: at one point he nearly becomes secretary to the exiled Trotsky in Mexico, the man of history and historicism who shares with Augie's other heroes the wish to navigate by the great stars. But the great stars are not quite enough for him, because there is also the matter of nature. Augie sees around him a great massed weight of human ideas, with as much bulk as the massing, in a world of endless random energy, of material and men, an exciting but excessive abundance of thought turned into life:

> There's too much of everything of this kind, *that's* come home to me, too much history and culture to keep track of, too many details, too much news, too much example, too much influence, too many guys to tell you to be as they are, and all this hugeness, abundance, turbulence, Niagara Falls torrent. Which who is supposed to interpret? Me? (p. 525)

It is this swamping, exciting mass of 'it' that becomes the point of anxiety for all of Bellow's later heroes, raising in new form the problem of trying to discover the human mean.

Augie's quest therefore takes him beyond the social and historical world and into nature, seeking to find the basis of his tenure there: 'It takes some of us a long time to find out what the price is of our being in nature, and what the facts are about your tenure', he reflects. 'How long it takes depends on how swiftly the social sugars dissolve' (p. 421). He tries to acquaint himself with biological and bodily laws, often in comic form (like the eagle-training session in Mexico), and with an openness far beyond that accessible to Joseph and Leventhal, both of whom are characterized by their suppression of emotional aspects of their lives. Augie struggles in sexual relationships and friendships, at the same time hoping to find a stillness somewhere that will afford access to life's 'axial lines', those angles of guidance and revelation where 'life can come together again and man be regenerated' (p. 524). But he is a comic hero, forced, like all Bellow's heroes, to mediate between the world of action and that of thought, to make some sense of the life constituted for him in the book. He ends, as he must, in contingency, knowing that no one is special, that mortality threatens, that there is no possession of anyone or anything, that man is both good and evil, that the historical amassing of the world and the anxiety it generates is real and cannot be refused. He acquires a chastened sense of history's powers, but also a 'mysterious adoration of what occurs'.

He has learned, in short, the passion for self-constitution that permits him to constitute the narrative, lets him write as a chastened comedian of possibility, celebrating 'the *animal ridens* in me, the laughing creature, forever rising up'. The laughter is against human hope, but also is that hope:

> . . . is the laugh at nature — including eternity — that it thinks it can win over us and the power of hope? Nah, nah! I think. It never will. But that possibly is the joke, on one or the other, and laughing is an enigma that includes both. (p. 617)

And this is exactly the enigma the book distils, as it looks both into the dark weighty claims of modern historical experience and the passions that might be expended against it.

*

But the claims of the material world do not leave Bellow's fiction, as *Seize the Day* (1956) went on to show. Indeed, after the contingent open style and comic abundance of *The Adventures of Augie March*, this could well be read as a step backward toward his earlier manner of writing. It is a tight novella set in New York over a very short time-span, a period of twenty-four hours, one seized day; and, like a short story, it moves toward one single dense instance of illumination. (Suitably it appeared in the American edition along with three of Bellow's best short stories, 'A Father to Be' (1955), 'Looking for Mr Green' (1951), 'The Gongaza Manuscripts' (1954), and his one-act play *The Wrecker*.) In *Seize the Day* an exact economy prevails, the story's world being created only as it impinges on its hero, in a sequence of instants. Likewise the title asserts this notion of instantaneousness, so opposite, in a sense, to Augie March's abundant inclusiveness. But this book, too, is a comedy, exploring the relationship between an absurd human being and an act of affirmation; indeed it has been rightly seen as a classic story of the Jewish *Schlemiel* (the type of whom Jewish lore has it, 'If he went into the hat business, babies would be born without heads'), the clown of failure who also contains a virtuous suffering compassion.

Tommy is certainly a superfluous man, an ex-actor who has appropriately worked for seven years as an 'extra', in films, a clown-victim for whom nothing ever goes quite right, who is tugged together out of chaos. His Hollywood ambitions, career in salesmanship and marriage are all on the rocks; he is at the mercy of an accusing father and an exploiting wife. There is a wild absurdity about his body and clothes ('He liked to wear good clothes, but once he had put it on each article appeared to go its own way' (*SD*, p. 9)). On this one day, just before Yom Kippur, he is drowning in his stock of experience – a middle-aged semi-failure in a seedy hotel who still just hopes, like the pigeon he sees beyond the hotel window, to fly. Yet he knows himself to be a clumsy animal, needing help, a man of sorrows from whom everything goes and to whom nothing comes back, but who dreams beyond his own imperfection of a larger body and a larger soul. Already a man of ten false decisions, he is about to make another, by entrusting his money to the commercial manipulations of Dr Tamkin, a superb figure of the charlatan, a psychic adviser and classic confidence man who is able to see into the uncertainties and contentions of Tommy's burdened soul, offers to lead him through the money-markets to spiritual release, and gives him the advice he wishes to hear: 'The past is no good to us. The future is full of anxiety. Only the present is real – the here-and-now. Seize the day' (p. 72). A man of love must have help in a world like this, if he is to transform soul into social power, to take, as Tamkin puts it, a 'specimen risk'.

For all its tight economy, *Seize the Day* is very much in Bellow's new manner, a story of man as a suffering joker divided between the practical material world and a larger world of being. It is one of his most poised pieces of writing, tonally very exact and developing according to elaborate metaphorical codes, careful analogies and parallelisms, a matching of experience in objects and nature. The secondary characters are all aspects of Tommy's quest – the stifling father, the exploiting wife, the various false guides of his life, like his corrupt agent Maurice Venice. Its comedy is metaphysical and complex, especially as it is distilled in the figure of Tamkin, the sage-like reality-instructor, the man who hints he has been one of the Detroit Purple Gang, headed a mental clinic, invented an unsinkable ship, and 'understands what gives'. A reader of everything, author of the self-help poem 'Mechanism vs Functionalism: Ism vs Hism', he promotes 'spontaneous emotions, open receptors and free impulses'. Tommy is the trapped comic victim, the clown of desire imprisoned in the biological facts of his existence, burdened with his 'inescapable self':

> The spirit, the peculiar burden of his existence, lay on him like an accretion, a load, a lump. In any moment of quiet, when sheer fatigue prevented him from struggling, he was apt to feel this mysterious weight, this growth or collection of nameless things which it was the business of his life to carry about. That must be what a man is for. (p. 44)

But that self is the treasure, if it can be not a 'pretender soul', trapped in the social mechanism and so existing only in a state of suffering, but a true soul, a larger body, that can go with joy. And it is this that Tamkin offers to release, by using money to go beyond money, to pass beyond a stock-market 'killing' to a curing, a more than material state. Tamkin displays Bellow's gift for superb character invention, and is the forerunner of many such figures; between them, Tommy and Tamkin and their metaphysical chatter make the book a moral farce.

But it is a serious farce, as we follow the essential metaphor – Tommy's motion from 'drowning', constriction, congestion to its final release in an opening of the heart. It comes through a strange path: Tamkin leads Tommy through the massed, over-whelming city to a brokerage office, where he is to make his 'killing' on the lard market, and restore his battered fortunes. Of course the money is lost; so is Tamkin, who promptly disappears. Materially destroyed, Tommy seems defeated. But Tamkin is guru as well as charlatan; he has always suggested that his promises are more than material, that through counter-feit meanings we might come to a humane truth. So it is appropriately the glimpsed figure of Tamkin, or someone like him, who leads Tommy to his final step. Chasing the trickster, he jostles through the crowds to find himself in a funeral parlour, where an unknown corpse lies in its bodily mystery, the ultimate double. Tommy, drowning in his unreleased tears and the watery grave of his circumstances, weeps at last over the stranger-corpse, tears that take him, we are told, 'deeper than sorrow, through torn sobs and cries toward the con-summation of his heart's ultimate need' (p. 126). Such is the precise economy of the story that this is both its metaphorical and its humanistic outcome – Tommy's weeping is the final concentrating image of the chokings and drownings that have been threatening him, and a sacral resolution of the chaos of his so far unseized day.

His final release may thus be supposed to be his restoration, his atonement, his discovery of his own mortality but also of its potential. Tommy weeps for the body of another, and his own insufficient and debased body; he weeps, too, to find that that 'killing' to which he has devoted his day has a meaning, being part of the compromised struggle that life makes with lifeless-ness. He weeps also to find himself a part of the city's moving crowd, a crowd to which he has been helplessly trying to reach; and he weeps to discover the mortality that makes the living and the dead into one community, making life senseless but making living activity into a value, because it is simply all there is. At the same time the scene trembles, characteristically and comically, on the brink; Tommy is the comic mourner at the wrong funeral, mistakenly assumed by the crowd to be a close relative of the dead man ('The man's brother, maybe?') even though they are not alike. Tommy remains absurd to the last, yet it is the condition of absurdity that now comes to recognition; it is what we share, for there *is* a meaning in our lumbering body, our mortal existence, our clownlike status in the material world. The luminous moment on which the story ends both affirms and questions that daily absurdity. Thus, rather like Augie, Tommy, though absurd, is potential, and moves comically through an insufficient world to a humane outcome. And it is indeed this possibility of comic humanism that, with these novels of the 1950s, comes to seem the prime matter of enquiry in Bellow's work.

*

With *The Adventures of Augie March* and *Seize the Day*, Bellow seemed to have undertaken a new enterprise in comic perception. The first book uses autobiographical, picaresque, adventurous contingency to explore both the inescapability of history and the possibility of its dissolution in redemptive laughter; the second uses a method of poetic metaphysical distillation to dissolve the contingent material world into absurd tears. With his next book, *Henderson the Rain King* (1959), Bellow went on to draw the two enterprises together, mixing spacious picaresque construction and metaphorical concentration in a novel that seeks – just like its first-person narrator, Eugene Henderson – for 'grandeur', but seeks it in a mythic intensity and a symbolistic method.

Henderson the Rain King is indeed a book of enormous rhetorical and narrative extravagance; like *The Adventures of Augie March*, it is structured on a capacious self-narrating and a free and open pattern of 'adventures'. But, where Augie passes through a world of loosely enlarging social experience with metaphoric potential, Henderson explores *his* vitalistic desires in a landscape that is quickly transformed from one of social and historical specificity, from the amassed stuff of contemporary America or Europe, into legendary time and mythic space, so that the laws of ordering function differently. The bulk of the novel is placed in the landscape of an imaginary Africa (a continent Bellow had not visited) which is deliberately made prehistoric rather than historic, a world beyond human footprints, a place where 'all travel is mental'. And where Bellow's earlier books amend but respect the laws of realism and naturalism, *Henderson the Rain King* moves in another direction that also has deep roots in the history of American fiction, into the form of 'romance'.

'Romance' was the classic American Transcendentalist form, the mode of a fiction preoccupied neither by laws of realism deriving from social specificity nor by the prevailing rules of the normal. It was, said Nathaniel Hawthorne, the place where the actual and the imaginary might meet, each imbued with the properties of the other, and where a displayed fictional invention, a taste for the fantastic *and* the self-reflexive, might contend with and qualify the claim of empirical fact, the life of social and historical existence. It was a structure for enunciating American romantic idealism, but in modern fiction it has undergone a significant revival as a result of modern scepticism about realism. Robert Scholes has noted that one of the reasons for the solvency of realism in contemporary writing, and the movement of the novel toward what he calls 'fabulation' – to modes of romance, fantasy, myth, grotesquerie and self-conscious fictionality – has been the need to depict the power and dominance of the inner life.[13]

The comment applies well to *Henderson the Rain King*, a book that steps out of the social and historical world and at the same time evokes many of the romances of the past (it has appropriately been compared with Melville's *Moby Dick* (1851), where Ishmael likewise leaves the dull, land-based life of debasement and irritability to begin his quest into nature; and with Mark Twain's *A Connecticut Yankee at King Arthur's Court* (1889), where that romantic quest soon turns toward destruction). *Henderson the Rain King* likewise leaves realism behind in order to quest for 'reality' – Henderson describes himself as a man who, learning that T. S. Eliot's nightingale tells us that humankind cannot stand very much reality, asks how much *un*reality it can stand ('I fired that question right back of the nightingale. So what if reality may be terrible? It's better than what we've got' (p. 100)). The difference between classic American romance and Henderson's quest is that his is certainly comic and to a considerable degree parodic, and so needs reading very differently.

Bellow's achievement in the book is that, without ponderousness or over-assertion, he can provide the elaborate constituents of a modern journey into spirit, nature and culture, and so create a texture of contemporary mythography; at the same time he can ironize such a romantic and self-vaunting enterprise. Henderson is thus conceived – by Bellow and by himself, as first-person narrator – in the grand manner. He suffers none of the outward victimizations of Bellow's earlier heroes, being his first non-Jewish central figure, a millionaire of Anglo-Saxon Protestant stock who is recipient to a large heritage of wealth, historical responsibility and social service, a massive access to the history of American and western culture. His utterance is a vaunt, and extravagance is the functional state of his being. He has an excess of body, with a height of 6 ft 4 ins, a weight of 230 lbs; his face is, as he says, like Grand Central Station, or an unfinished church; he has 'the bulk of a football player and the colour of a gypsy'; he clothes himself in the clothes of farce. His inward life matches; he is, he says, to suffering what Gary is to smoke. He is a man of excess over-stated in nature:

> The sun is like a great roller and flattens the grass. Beneath this grass the earth may be filled with carcasses, yet that distracts nothing from a day like this, for they have become human and the grass is thriving. When the air moves the brilliant flowers move too in the dark green beneath the

trees. They burst against my open spirit because I am in the midst of this in the red violet dressing gown from the Rue de Rivoli bought on the day when Frances spoke the word divorce. I am there and am looking for trouble. (p. 31)

Disconcertingly positioned in relation to others, to society, objects and the natural world, rough, violent, physical, power-ful, disoriented and soul-searching, Henderson is a meta-physical comedian, a supernatural bumbler with aspirations for his soul, a psycho-braggart speaking the great romantic vaunt of the Self.

So his wealth and scale, his violence and his frantic and grandiose marrying, loving and soul-searching, his heavy hand holding the delicate violin he wishes to play, all translate into a discourse that moves freely from vernacular confession to biblical incantation, and is the most marvellous quality of the book. His soul as readily to hand as his clothes, Henderson's language becomes a remarkable device for mediating an action that is equally extravagant and giving it intellectual and mythic possibilities and pretensions. His character is deliberately in-tended to call forth an analogous world of absurdity in experi-ence: as he says, 'a damned fool going out into the world is bound and fated to encounter damned fool phenomena' (p. 59). And so, in Africa, he does, for Bellow invents a continent bereft of its more familiar contents and replaced by two contrasting states of history, culture, and psychic relation to nature, and these likewise function both mythically and com-ically.

Henderson is indeed, as Bellow once said, 'an absurd seeker after high qualities'; his adventures both evoke basic myths or archetypes and present themselves as the stuff of eclectic anthropological and cosmic farce. Like all first-person narra-tors, Henderson is hard to measure, and the book has been very variously read. But Henderson's egocentric story of spiritual hunger, his endless *I want, I want*, his drive to burst his spirit's sleep, is clearly a central part of Bellow's own mythic world. It is a world that starts in society, departs it, and returns to it;

where *Henderson the Rain King* most differs from the other novels is in the scale granted to the hero and the degree to which the novel is created as an outward map of his inward psychic terrain.

Above all Henderson is a comic imperial hero appropriate to his time, that of the Eisenhower regnum, the season of material superpowerdom. He recognizes that it is the destiny of his generation of Americans to get out into the world to try to find life's wisdoms, and this means a step from his present material condition, which is that of a 'trophy':

> A man like me may become something like a trophy. Washed, clean, and dressed in expensive garments. Under the roof is insulation; on the windows thermopane; on the floors carpeting; and on the carpets furniture, and on the furniture covers, and on the cloth covers plastic covers; and wallpaper and drapes! All is swept and garnished. And who is in the midst of this? Who is sitting there? Man! That's who it is, man! (p. 26)

He belongs to a world stuffed to excess with materials and goods, but feels detached from his antecedents and culture, heir to a meaningless inheritance, 'a displaced person'. 'Nobody truly occupies a station in life any more', he reflects. 'There are mostly people who feel they occupy the place that belongs to another by rights' (p. 35).

Society is again a lunatic contemporary prison, a place of chaotic rush and inhuman madness, creating a dislocated or debased image of the self: so, as an act of deliberate cultural sacrilege, he farms pigs, making great profits while feeling himself as debased as his animals. He is energetic but aimless, powerful but dissipating power, moving toward entropy. Like previous Bellow heroes, if on a characteristically larger scale, he finds that social existence generates depression and rage. His marriage is a disaster, and whenever he goes among people there is, he says, 'the devil to pay'. He accepts that he lives in an age of madness, and that 'to expect to be untouched by madness is a form of madness. But the pursuit of sanity can be a form of madness, too' (p. 27). And it is his rage that brings about his break with society; losing his temper with his family one morning at breakfast, he rages so loudly that it frightens and kills the old lady who comes in to cook his meals. He reads this as the final lesson in his debasement, evidence of the way he disturbs and is disturbed by the surrounding environment, is unfit to live among men. So, threatened too with pointless death, he leaves a note on the corpse (*Do not disturb*), and sets out, a man who has ruined 'the original piece of goods issued to me and was travelling to find a remedy' (p. 74), from the social to the pre-social world.

The Africa he travels to is of course classic mythic ground for the western mind; his journey calls up the history of safari, exploration and buried treasure; Livingstone, Hemingway, Tarzan and 'She', the heart of darkness, the waste land of barbarism secreted in civilization, 'Mr Kurtz – he dead'. But a damned fool indeed encounters damned fool phenomena, and Bellow's is a mock-Africa, anthropologically dense and allusive but populated with African absurdists and Dr Tamkins, black gurus in pursuit themselves of much the same natural, anthropological and determinist lore that preoccupies Henderson's own abundant mind. Africa promptly looks to Henderson like 'the ancient bed of mankind'; the land is all 'simplified and splendid, and I felt I was entering the past – the real past, no history or junk like that' (p. 46). In fact history is not so easily escaped; the two tribes he presently encounters represent two fundamental versions of the relationship between man and nature, myth and history. He travels through the desert with a Christian African guide, Romilayu, who takes him first to the Arnewi, a peaceable tribe of cattle-raisers who appear to live in a prehistoric Golden Age. Their language contains no oppositions, and they live by an unambitious goodness, removed from Henderson's desire to burst his spirit's sleep. Even so, Henderson has little trouble making his metaphysical hungers understood, and most of those he meets are in some fashion conspirators in his soul-searching; even the animals conspire with his psychic needs and ambitions. So, too, does the weather; he arrives in a time of drought, when the cattle are dying from the pollution of their water tank by frogs; the Arnewi's religion of acceptance forbids them to intervene.

As with Mark Twain's Hank Morgan (in *A Connecticut Yankee At King Arthur's Court*) Henderson's innocent American desire for service is aroused: 'I thought, this will be one of those mutual aid deals; where the Arnewi are irrational I'll help them; and where I'm irrational they'll help me' (p. 83). Custom first demands he wrestle with the chief, whom he defeats with his strength, and meet the queen, Willatale, blind in one eye, as Bellow's Sammler (*Mr Sammler's Planet*) will be, and similarly a repository of transhistorical wisdom. She accepts Henderson and tells him that he possesses *grun-tu-molani*, 'man wants to live', the life-force. Feeling he is on the right track, he decides to use Yankee technology and blow the frogs out of the tank with home-made explosives; he blows up both frogs and tank. The drought has already been recognized as internal ('As we turned away I felt as though that cistern of problem water with its algae and its frogs had entered me, occupying a square space in my interior, and sloshing around as I moved' (p. 60)) and the disaster is Henderson's too. Unable to acquiesce in the given, able to counter stagnation only with excess vitality and technique, he has to leave in disgrace and humiliation, 'having demolished both the water and my hopes. From now I'd never learn more about the *grun-tu-molani*' (p. 106).

But his unwilling Vergil, Romilayu, leads him to a second tribe, the Wariri ('chillun darkness', says Romilayu), who were once linked to the Arnewi but now live in a different historical and psychological stage, belonging to the fallen timebound world, an age of violence, action and change. Where the Arnewi manifest a 'female' peacefulness and acceptance, the Wariri manifest a 'male' energy and force. The Arnewi are associated with cattle; the Wariri beast is the lion, and culture and nature are in endless psychic struggle.[14]

This is more appropriate territory for Henderson, and the place of his chief adventures. The Wariri – who have a more complex social system, carry guns, and have a kind of police and immigration service – capture and interrogate him and place him in a room with a corpse, confronting him with his deepest anxiety, that of death; he copes by disposing of the body in a ravine. This is a test of strength; the Wariri have a use for Henderson's excessive, undirected energy. Instead of accepting the drought, they have a rain-making ritual to break it – to 'prime the pumps of the firmament', as their king, Dahfu, puts it. Part of the ritual involves lifting a heavy wooden goddess, Mummah, from one spot to another; after the tribal strongman fails, Henderson, feeling use for his strength at last, asks permission to undertake the task and, in what is effectively a moment of sexual mastery over the idol, he succeeds and feels renewed:

> I was so gladdened by what I had done that my whole body was filled with soft heat, with soft and sacred light. . . . My spirit was awake and welcomed life anew. Damn the whole thing! Life anew! I was still alive and kicking and I had the old *grun-tu-molani*. (p. 181)

Spirit and world seem to meet in a function; part of Henderson's quest is over. But there is the question of social service: Henderson now becomes Sungo, the tribal rain king, being stripped, thrown into a water tank and made part of a shrieking dance as the rain obligingly falls. Above all he must become concerned with the political position of King Dahfu, educated in Syria, and 'a genius of my own mental type'. Dahfu is one of Bellow's richest versions of the wise if sometimes dangerous instructor, who often appears to Bellovian heroes, a man of thought, learning and extreme applications; and, like other heroes of legend, Henderson now has tasks to perform.

Dahfu has evolutionist psychological theories, a compound of Lamarck and Wilhelm Reich, believing that the body originates in the brain, so that man may create his physiology, or change it:

> what he was engrossed by was a belief in the transformation of human materials, that you could work either way, either

from the rind to the core or from the core to the rind; the flesh influencing the mind, the mind influencing the flesh, back again to the mind, back once more to the flesh. . . . For him it was not enough that there might be disorders of the body that originated in the brain. *Everything* originated there. 'Although I do not wish to reduce the stature of our discussion', he said, 'yet for the sake of example the pimple on a lady's nose may be her own idea, accomplished by a conversion at the solemn command of her psyche; even more fundamentally the nose itself, though part hereditary, is part also her own idea.' (pp. 220–1)

And he urges Henderson to adapt the 'exceptional amalgam of violent forces' in him by introducing him to a lioness he keeps in the palace, a figurative equivalent of 'the noble' which will have its turn in the world. He explains that Henderson, in isolating himself, becoming *self*-conscious, has grown contracted, whereas the lioness 'does not take issue with the inherent. Is one hundred per cent within the given' (p. 245). Henderson's experience of instruction with the lioness, the killing beast totally unified and in itself, generates scenes of wonderful invention within a remarkably inventive book, a book which metaphorically turns on the legendary equivalence between animal life and human states of being. But before the lessons are complete, accident dissolves the apparently profitable instruction; Dahfu is killed by a wild lion on a ritual lion hunt, and reveals finally that Henderson is his successor – and that when he loses the power to carry Mummah and satisfy the harem of wives he will be sacrificed, and hence that savagery is not capable of being mastered but involves lasting violence. Henderson's situation returns to extremity; he sees that Dahfu too has not resolved the problem of relating energy to communal task.

Henderson escapes from the Wariri, taking with him the lion cub thought to be Dahfu's soul, and a concept of human nobility drawn from him, which he utters to Romilayu:

We're supposed to think nobility is unreal. But that's just it.

The illusion is on the other foot. They make us think we crave more and more illusions. Why, I don't crave illusions at all. They say, Think big. Well, that's baloney of course, another business slogan. But greatness! That's another thing altogether. Oh, greatness! Oh, God! Romilayu, I don't mean inflated, swollen, false greatness. . . . But the universe itself being put into us, it calls out for scope. The eternal is bonded onto us. It calls out for its share. (p. 297)

And, in what is to be a characteristic ending, the path of instruction has itself to be amended: the lessons taken have been to a degree mock lessons. Flying home across the Atlantic, accompanied by the lion cub, reminder of nobility sacrificed to society, and an orphan boy he has met on the flight, his final twin, he realizes that he must settle for his own nature, closer to the fairground bear, that sad humorist, than the lion.

Thus, as before, the novel ends on a contained and measured possibility; Henderson is now no longer matched to the pigs with which he began, nor to the cattle or the lion, but to his own comic shambling largeness. Warrior and female principle, violence and gentleness reconcile; the world contains lasting traces that are more than single occasions. Henderson has found a print in nature to attach himself to:

if corporeal things are an image of the spiritual and visible objects are renderings of invisible ones, then Smolak [the fairground bear he had once worked with] and I were outcasts together, two humorists before the crowd, but brothers in our souls – I embeared by him, and he probably humanized by me . . . something deep was already inscribed on me. (p. 316)

Landing in Newfoundland, Henderson, knowing his imprint, runs with bear and child round the plane, 'leaping, leaping, pounding and tingling over the pure white lining of the grey Arctic silence' (p. 318). It closes on a sense of freedom, a celebration of stark created nature; but also a sense of the conditioned and the bonded. Like Augie before him and Herzog after, Henderson enters the kingdom of knowledge which contains both process and biology and those eternal traces – the limits and the possibilities of self-creation.

Henderson in fact concludes the book as Bellow's most affirmative hero, to the end the abundant comedian of his own self-assertion. Bellow once spoke of Henderson's quest as 'a remedy for his anxiety over death . . . the indeterminate and indefinite anxiety, which most of us accept as the condition of life which he is foolhardy enough to resist.' His struggle has been against 'cosmic coldness'; yet, in the Newfoundland cold, he finds a state of joy in which he can run freely.[15]

It is an ending that Leslie Fiedler has called one of 'unearned euphoria', and it promotes certain doubts. What, though, sustains the lyric note to the end is Bellow's own note of comic metaphysics, which conducts Henderson – with his sense that one must live a thing before one knows it, and that visible objects are the renderings of invisible ones – into a new and promising state of living to know. It is this engaged space between the lyric and the comic, manifesting itself both as metaphysics and wit, that gives Bellow the tones of a major novelist. Henderson's progress through the kingdom of nature, through a world where animals measure out the stuff of human potential, where single instances leave lasting traces, where a commanding biology can be transliterated into an endless becoming, is an extraordinary conceit. The mythic intent makes it very much a book of the fifties: a decade obsessed with the hope that the imagination might generate at last the saving fable, the tale of the waste land redeemed, the desert of civilization watered by some humanist or metaphysical discovery. But the myth both asserts and mocks itself, takes on a neo-parodic form; and it is the method of comic fabulation, of expansive and pyrotechnic farce, of absurdity finding a path to human measurement, that makes *Henderson the Rain King* so strangely notable a novel.

4

THE SIXTIES NOVELS: 'HERZOG' AND 'MR SAMMLER'S PLANET'

We love apocalypses too much, and crisis ethics and florid extremism with its thrilling language. Excuse me, no. I've had all the monstrosity I want. We've reached an age in the history of mankind when we can ask about certain persons, 'What is this Thing?' No more of that for me – no, no! I am simply a human being, more or less. (*Herzog*)

By the end of the 1950s, Saul Bellow had the look of being the exemplary novelist of the decade – the writer who expressed with the greatest subtlety and intensity the tensions and estrangements of an age and a social order that both liberated and confined, released and dehumanized, and who registered its disturbed sensations of material excess and spiritual scarcity, its feelings of mind and consciousness disordered and crowded by intellectual excess, urban pressure and moral anxiety. Bellow pointed to the sense of madness but seemed to lead it toward recovery, toward appropriate affirmations that did not overlook the dangers of either an excess of self or a shrouding and shrinking of it, but found some Whitmanesque collusion possible between the single separate person and the corporate mass. The whole point of his work seemed to be that the claims both of the hungering single psyche and of the disorderly public chaos of mind could find attachment, if only through an avaricious scepticism that made intelligent doubt and a kind of fervent mental madness the only negotiable way to such a humanist possibility. *Henderson the Rain King*, written as the 1950s ended, offered his strongest assertion yet that the limits set on self-creation do not obstruct the hope of transcendental discovery. But, as the sixties started, it was not hard to see a rising doubt in Bellow's contemporaries. Kennedy's election appeared to coincide with a great, inventive wave of new cultural reckoning, a fresh burst of creation; but it was sharply touched with anxiety and despair. Those novelists who turned to contemporary history reported it, as did Joseph Heller and Kurt Vonnegut, in terms of humanism defeated; the novel of irrational dissent flourished, as in William S. Burroughs and Norman Mailer; the stupefying *un*reality of contemporary reality outran, said Philip Roth, all fictional invention.

'The power of public life has become so threatening that private life cannot maintain the pretence of its importance', Bellow noted himself in 'Some Notes on Recent American Fiction' (1963), in which he examined several of the best novels of the Kennedy years, including John Updike's *Rabbit, Run* (1960), J. F. Powers's *Morte d'Urban* (1962), Bruce J. Friedman's *Stern* (1962) and Philip Roth's *Letting Go* (1962), and reflected on their direction. Invoking the title of Wylie Sypher's admirable work in modern intellectual and literary history, *Loss of the Self in Modern Art and Literature* (1962), he noticed the way in which a fiction that saw a world divided between an overpowering reality and a chaotic fleeting self now dominated American writing – so that it was now possible for European readers to find in it an instinctive or unexamined confirmation of the most depressed interpretations and philosophies of modern history. It appeared that twentieth-century American experience made the rejection of Rousseauesque ideas of the Unique Self virtually necessary; novelists either moved toward the privatization of the self, a 'hoarding of spiritual valuables', or they came to 'reject and despise the Self', assaulting individualism and humanism, as in Sartre, Beckett and Burroughs. Bellow went on to question this 'unearned bitterness', this instinctive acceptance of waste land beliefs, remarking:

> What is truly curious about it is that often the writer automatically scorns contemporary life. He bottles its stinks

68

artistically. But, seemingly, he does not need to study it. It is enough for him that it does not allow his sensibilities to thrive, that it starves his instincts for nobility or spiritual qualities. (*NT*, p. 62)

He grants some justice to the lineage of despair, seeing that it is consequential on much fundamental modern thought from Romanticism onward. But, he argues, modern life simply extends the mystery of the human self, which is not what it was once thought, but which demands a revised measurement and judgement. The need is not for the reiteration of the Romantic solutions but the extension of the enquiry, Bellow suggests; thereby proposing the project of his next novel, *Herzog* (1964), perhaps his most conclusively expressed and densest book.

So, where *Henderson the Rain King* seems very explicitly addressed to the fifties, *Herzog* seems very explicitly addressed to the sixties. The comic picaresque, releasing the hero into romantic self-enquiry, will no longer serve; this is because Herzog's adventures are essentially those of the mind, but also because that mind is constrained, in interaction with a social universe at odds with it – Bellow's ever-changing but ever-present world of the modern city in its apocalyptic wildness, which becomes an external referent for Herzog's inner despair. Indeed the novel may be read as an exploration of the compelling justification *for* a lore of despair, an enterprise Bellow then seeks to counteract with experiential *and* fictional discovery. World and consciousness are emotionally and formally at odds; disintegration and madness are the theme. Moses Herzog – the name comes from a marginal character in Joyce's *Ulysses*, a text never remote from this novel – is scholar and madman, a student of Romanticism in a world where romantic indulgences have become fashionable five-cent syntheses, the easy solutions of self in a world of hyperabundance. And it is a book of such abundances, for in a sense Herzog goes mad with intellectual splendour, living in a state of endless mental strife where he argues with most of the available interpreters of the universe.

Indeed it is largely this that generates his 'instability', his fervent mental and social action, his wonderful letters, his incessant comic argument with his 'reality-instructors', his attempt to re-encounter and re-interpret the chaotic, amassed data of his past and his present existence. Bellow described the theme of the book as 'the imprisonment of the individual in a shameless and impotent privacy',[16] but the way out of this is, again, the comic will to become, which is once more the object of Bellow's attention — 'comic' because Herzog is a 'suffering joker' in whom self and community, reason and desire, romantic self-knowledge and contingent understanding, will never stop warring. And this is true within Herzog's intellectual life itself; he is a scholar of Romanticism, whose work aims to overturn 'the last of the Romantic errors about the uniqueness of the self' (p. 45) and so challenge the old western Faustian ideology. Yet he himself is embroiled deeply in the logic of despair.

But Herzog's is not simply a personal but a historical anguish, an anguish in relation to our modern circumstance, as the text tells us:

> And why? Because he let the entire world press on him. For instance? Well, for instance, what it means to be a man. In a city. In a century. In transition. In a mass. Transformed by science. Under organized power. Subject to tremendous controls. In a condition caused by mechanization. After the late failure of radical hopes. In a society that was no community and devalued the person. Owing to the multiplied power of numbers that made the self negligible. Which spent military billions against foreign enemies but would not pay for order at home, which permitted savagery and barbarism in its own great cities. (p. 208)

Not only the intellectual heritage on which he draws but the surrounding world which intrudes upon and insists on its presence with him point therefore in the direction of madness. Relations are perverted, indifference rules, suffering is widespread, emptiness is common, all guides, even the most intimate and domestic, are negative tutors, his own social, ethnic, sexual and intellectual experience emphasizes loss and marginality; the history of alienation makes sense to him. Madness is its logical distillation, and so is a psychic act of violent revolt against the emotional persecutions, the damaging boredoms, the false interpretations, the swamping city. Surrounding him is a world of mass and sign, of spurious cultural objects and images, realms of offered being that provide elegant masks but not real substances and investitures. 'In this new age of multitudes, self-awareness tends to reveal us to ourselves as monsters' (p. 171), Herzog writes in one of the many letters he addresses not just to the 'fictional' characters of the novel, but to American public figures and the illustrious living and dead thinkers of the world, with whom he is in endless unanswered communication. His map of transaction thus includes the historically present society, as he sees it, and the massive intellectual stock of Romantic bourgeois ideology, and all this makes for the largeness of the book.

Yet at the same time the existing maps are not sufficient. Behind Herzog is indeed the great Romantic wisdom, and the conflict it secretes — between man as potentially free spirit ('to Tolstoi, freedom is entirely personal. That man is free whose condition is simple, truthful — real' (p. 169) and man as historically and circumstantially conditioned (Herzog recalls Hegel, who sees that the essence of human life is derived from 'History, memory — that is what makes us human, that, and our knowledge of death' (*H*, p. 169)). To reconcile the elements is the drive of the book (making its emphasis markedly different from *Henderson the Rain King*), but the offered solutions — alienated selfhood, urgent political actor demystifying the 'false consciousness' of the free self — become in turn false or five-cent syntheses; for his, Herzog is prepared to pay more. Synthesis itself is a comic posture, a function of our metaphysical absurdity; history, massed alike in the city and Herzog's own mind, where the old ideas of genius have become the canned goods of intellectuals ('Do we need *theories* of pain and anguish?'), has itself become farce:

71

I fall upon the thorns of life; I bleed. And what next? I get laid, I take a short holiday, but very soon after I fall upon those same thorns with gratification in pain or suffering in joy – who knows what the mixture is! (p. 214)

Herzog, seeking to redistil history and our idea of it, displacing the Christian view of it as 'crisis', challenging the utopian version which offers an idyll to compare with the world as is, trying to find 'a new angle on the modern condition, showing how life could be lived by renewing universal connection, overturning the last of the Romantic errors about the uniqueness of the Self' (p. 45), has an urgent Becoming to achieve. But he does – if out of accident and contingency, the experience of the world as it impinges on the consciousness – avert his 'merely aesthetic critique of modern history', accept a changed relation of mental and social to natural being, find a moment of balanced tenure.

*

Herzog's is a large crisis; what is notable is that it puts not only his own mind but the formal act of expression of the book under enormous pressure, driving Bellow's work in a new direction. The book's actual narrative line is simple and easy to summarize: it is the story of one man's sufferings after his second marriage has broken up, as he moves toward divorce in several senses, the story of, as he says, 'how I rose from humble origins to complete disaster', a mock *Bildungsroman*. He is a Jewish-American scholar born of immigrant parents who, originally poor and unsuccessful, finally achieve business success late in life, allowing him to live financially secure as an able and respected intellectual. He marries, first, a conventional Jewish wife of orderly and classical tastes, Daisy, who confines him and whom he divorces; then, after an episode with a complaisant Japanese mistress, he marries the vastly more wilful and various Madeleine, a Catholic convert of extravagant tastes and intellectual ambitions. She finally leaves him to go and live with his best friend, who has been cuckolding him, keeping the daughter of the marriage. It is here the dominant

72

present of the narrative begins, concentrating on a short period of late spring and summer after the marriage break-up, when Herzog, accused by Madeleine of being insane, begins to accept the accusation. Isolated and suffering, he performs a succession of distracted and fragmentary acts which make him perceive his own attitudes, behaviour, family, past, sexuality, the city, his Jewish and his American history. Already disposed to eccentricity, he grows odder, treating his friends strangely, and writing letters in his mind to many correspondents, from Eisenhower to Spinoza ('*Thoughts not causally connected were said by you to cause pain. I find that is indeed the case*' (p. 189)) and Heidegger ('*Dear Doktor Professor Heidegger, I should like to know what you mean by the expression "the fall into the quotidian." When did this fall occur? Where were we standing when it happened?*' (p. 55)).

Still involved with his own marriage and cuckolding, he goes from his home in New York to the city of his growing up, Chicago (*Herzog* is indeed a tale of two cities), to save his daughter who has been left, he is told, outside the house by the wife and lover; he also means to kill the couple. He visits the old home, recalls his Jewish past, obtains his father's gun, and arrives at the house of the lovers. But abstract idea is dispelled by actuality; he watches the lover tenderly bathe the child. Instead he takes the child out in his car, and is involved in a minor accident, one of those transforming accidents that, asserting contingency's claim, frequently redirect the Bellovian plot. The police find the gun and he is briefly goaled for its possession; he is then freed, and the failure of his attempt to put his own life straight, and the disclosures of reality he has found on the way, send him to his house in Ludeyville, in the Berkshires, the old Transcendentalist landscape of Hawthorne and Melville. Here he resolves his ambiguities, or rather becomes 'much better at ambiguities'. He apparently recovers sanity in a state of unsteady pastoral, withdrawn but expectant, having 'at this time . . . no messages for anyone. Nothing', sufficed to be in human occupancy, in a state of mental and psychic stasis, though the arrest seems temporary, and he is just about to receive his philoprogenitive recent mistress. He has evidently discovered that experience and habit are deeper than ideas, that 'human life is far subtler than any of its models', that chance events and knowings are greater than all syntheses, that deeper connections exist below the fragmentary, and cause no pain. He thus ends the book beyond thought and language, in a moment of silence, with his life feeling 'not irrationally but incomprehensibly filled'.

This then is the plot of *Herzog*, but to describe it does not display the form of the book. For in it the intellectual and artistic pressures with which it engages seem explicitly to be converted into formal problems. Though the method is third-person narration, the mode is confessional; there is dislocation of the pronoun and of time. Herzog's search for a meaningful existence indeed corresponds to Bellow's search for a form for the novel; its apparently loose construction and drift – it begins and ends at roughly the same point – are central to its theme of pattern drawn from patternlessness. The self uttered and turned into thought and ideas is likewise crucial to Herzog's anxiety and difficulty: 'I go after reality with language', says Herzog, 'I put my whole heart into these constructions, but they are constructions'. Herzog must deconstruct himself; so, to a degree, must the novel. If consciousness and world are indeed at odds, how may consciousness relate to world, and both to language? The book's method may indeed be close to what Lukács calls 'critical realism' – in that it asserts the substance of society, the truth of history – but it blurs the basis of discrimination between narrated hero and narrator. The extraordinary action of Herzog's well-funded but bizarre and drifting mind – struggling 'to make coherent sense' – is laid over a plot of experiences which must challenge his mental conceptions of 'reality' and yet be more than episodic contingency. Hence the problem of discovered pattern in Bellow's ending, which more than most has disconcerted his critics: a 'fatty sigh of middle-class contentment', said one, John Aldridge. It points to Herzog's and the book's temporary silence, insists on his and the text's luminosity; it offers itself in the transcendence of art and attaches that transcendence to a willing openness toward the eternal powers in the universe, to the holy sense. Its note is close to that of romantic modernism, rescuing weighty silence from chaos; but the novel remains sustainedly and magnificently comic, and to a point qualifies its own conclusive moment, placing stability in more lasting instabilities yet to be faced. It is the pattern of the unpatterned that Bellow had constituted in the book, offering it as Herzog's discovery and the novelist's mystery.

At the same time versions of reality are put into doubt. Herzog's struggle is with the 'reality-instructors', those who theorize a historical condition into existence; and, he recognizes, humankind lives mainly on perverted ideas. Herzog's initial acquiescence in madness ('If I am out of my mind, it's all right with me, thought Moses Herzog', the book begins) means that he is immediately presented as an alternative and unreliable witness who will none the less witness, and not only on the activity of his own consciousness but on the state of the age. What he is at odds with is not therefore society or history as such but the dominant mental conceptions which order and name these things, generating false relation between inner and outer worlds, suffering celebrated and made into stalemate. Certainly, in the world, mind has a place, but it also is derived; we are given the detailed history and economics of Herzog's own intellectual derivation. Yet how may we perceive or triumph over that from which we derive? *Herzog* is a historicist struggle with historicism, Romanticism's apocalyptic outcome. It is an apocalyptic novel about the defeat of florid apocalypse — a long mental quarrel, conducted from the position of madness, with the advocates of irrational romanticism, therapeutic syntheses, the life of alternated boredom and stimulation in the wasted city.

The brilliant quarrel is itself Herzog's alternative therapy; his vivid intellectual and emotional warfare drives the book, turning against himself, for there must also be inward victory over the masks and ruses of suffering he himself employs. Herzog's struggle with those who 'tout the void', his

75

explanation to a fellow scholar that 'the advocacy and praise of suffering takes us in the wrong direction and those of us who remain loyal to civilization must not go for it', his rejection of what he has called 'the cheap mental stimulants of Alienation, the cant and rant of pipsqueaks about Inauthenticity and Forlornness' (p. 324), is indeed a struggle with departments of his own being. In this sense Bellow asks the mind to master the mind – though the struggle, left by Romanticism, is also with irrational advocacies, the Dionysian stock. Bellow recognizes the classic Freudian concern: civilization survives only by suppressing desire. Hence the sexual plot of the novel is fundamentally important, and Herzog's own psychology of narcissism and of sado-masochistic sexual suffering, coupled with his persistent sense of sexuality as a form of human betrayal or irrational self-debasement, is a primary element of the book.

It is not hard to see that *Herzog* does not entirely resolve its own field of tension, that it finds suspension in ambiguity. Itself haunted by apocalyptic Splengerian anxieties (much as is Edward Albee's almost contemporary play, *Who's Afraid of Virginia Woolf?* (1962)), with the western world order defeated by irrational powers and feckless subjectivities, by the betraying id that dissipates the moral awareness and the sense of the claim of the extant world, with its 'glassy temporal light', it seeks to challenge the apocalyptics with which we have learned to interpret life. Questioning the Faustian ego, it moves toward a romantic transcendentalism. Challenging the modern waste land confessional, it comes close to it in form. Its achievement – and it is notable – is, however, to dismiss the obvious lore of the issues with which it deals, and avoid the obvious formal outcomes (the psycho-verbal collapse and the sexual exposure of Philip Roth's Peter Tarnopol or Portnoy, for example). Herzog finds his 'new angle on the modern condition', recognizes a vividness and worth in the world, finds equilibrium without librium, accepts diurnality and history, finds a hint of the patterned secret. We may doubt the ending in the rural playground of Ludeyville, with its natural transcendence and its pleasure-principle associations, and find it a conventional pastoral set outside the city and society where the anguish is made; similarly the surviving relationship with Ramona offers an abeyance of the sexual warfare which is part of Bellow's contemporary reality. But what we should value is Bellow's comprehensive grasping of the lore of modern anguish, and his concern with the odds set against Herzog's momentary composure. If Bellow rejects the indulgent alienations that have come from the legacy of nineteenth-century Romanticism and historicism, and which have been ritualized into the late twentieth-century model of man, alienated, bored and therapeutically hungry amid material wealth, he has also made his hero an exacting figure of alienation, living amid the intellectual, social, political and psychological bewilderments of the modern urban capitalist world.

*

That Bellow's writing was increasingly concerned with such bleak apprehensions was to be made yet more obvious by the publication of his next book, *Mosby's Memoirs, and Other Stories* (1968). Several of these were from the 1950s, and three of the six had been published in the American edition of *Seize the Day*, but two – 'The Old System' (1967) and 'Mosby's Memoirs' (1968) – were written after *Herzog* and continue some of its themes. In the first, Dr Braun, a biochemist, reaches back – as had, so importantly, Herzog – into his Jewish family past and found in it a spectacle of older harmony and vitality, remote from his science. At the same time the recognizes the power of 'the cold eye':

> Perhaps the cold eye was better. On life, on death. But, again, the cold of the eye would be proportional to the degree of heat within. But once humankind had grasped its own idea, that it was human and human through such passions, it began to exploit, to play, to disturb for the sake of creating disturbance, to make an uproar, a crude circus of feelings. (*MM*, p. 80)

Braun, and perhaps mankind, may now have reached an age of equilibrium where emotional heraldry is out and the cold eye is needed, to contemplate the stars and the molecular processes, the true heraldry we are left with. 'Mosby's Memoirs' also deals with detachment and irony; Mosby is an ageing diplomat in México writing his memoirs in the manner of mental strife, but with a Henry Adams-like third-person detachment. He is then disturbed by memories of Lustgarten, a Jewish farceur whose wife he had seduced in Paris by demonstrating her husband's absurdity. Mosby's rational detachment lasts until he visits a tomb at Mitla, and something then cracks in his calm. Both stories map essential elements in Bellow's writing, the conflict of mind and Jewish lushness, of comic engagement and detached irony, and these are the elements that come to dominate in Bellow's next, most anxious and apocalyptic novel, *Mr Sammler's Planet* (1970).

Mr Sammler's Planet is evidently a crisis book for a crisis year, 1969, the year of high radical passions and moonshot. Again it is Bellow's evident assumption that a dark history is in process: on earth, the cities decline, romantic and irrational passions run wild ('The thing evidently, as Mr Sammler was beginning to grasp, consisted in obtaining the privileges, and the free ways of barbarism, under the protection of civilized order, property rights, refined technological organization, and so on' (*MSP*, p. 8)), while in the larger cosmos human consciousness seems to be in some process of biological osmosis, adjusting to the move toward the planets. New York City is a Babelian waste, disorganized, crime-ridden, over-populated, lost, sexually barren; only evil appears to invigorate. Consciousness is overwhelmed by force, as in Henry Adams's model of the modern multiverse; beneath a surface of anarchistic pleasure is an underlayer of despair. Apocalyptics are everywhere, including the text itself: Sammler sees himself in a new late era hungering to break its own moulds, and Bellow's own sense of a world come to crisis is patent in the book's tone.

Of all his novels, *Mr Sammler's Planet* comes closest to being a late Yeatsian enterprise, as the novelist impersonates through his central character, an ancient survivor, part-blind, once dead, endurant yet almost post-human, the distanced cold eye

78

on life, on death, that is close to wise resignation. This sense of distance, of contemplating a city in a nature on a planet, of gazing from long historical time at cosmic space, permits another line of enquiry to manifest itself in the book. It tells, on the one hand, local stories of the city, of pickpockets, student revolt, violence, personality hunger, the breakdown of old Jewish ways, the dominance of ego-assertive sexuality; it expounds, on the other, a long neo-scientific enquiry into the biological and lapidary context of man. The old humanist enquiry about man and nature, man and cosmos, man and history, man and his genetic function, is played against the data of humane civilization and its erupting opposite. A stony planetary nature surrounds man and is his proper condition; and the question of the way in which the species is evolving through a world that seems both intellectually and culturally to be driving toward some massive, indifferent, post-humanist enterprise in the cosmos is the central vision of the book.

It is a large venture, an attempt at cosmic assessment – needed, says Sammler, because 'at the moment of launching from this planet to another something was ended, finalities were demanded, summaries' (pp. 222–3). Sammler, the world citizen, is thus given the historical and temporal competence for such summaries. It is appropriate that this ancient one-eyed figure should have participated in the complicated history of modern European civilization, and in the course of this had been acquainted with H. G. Wells, on whom he is vaguely writing a book. Wells ended in despair and irony, and Sammler's one advantage – if advantage it is – over his subject is to have seen some of the presaged disasters, the counterforce to civilized society, the Auschwitz as well as the Bloomsbury. Auschwitz haunts and qualifies our concept of civilization, as many writers since the Second World War have asserted; Bellow encounters this proposition in the book and makes Sammler into a fundamental post-holocaust voice. So, far more displaced than Herzog, a true experiencer of the modern apocalypse, having come out of a German grave and committed his own killings, he carries with him the dark ambiguity in inherited culture, the double burden both of civilized European intensities and theories *and* the knowledge of their outcomes, the explicit experience of their irrational obverse which is also their consequence in the disorder and genocide of the death camps. Sammler is, in a sense, a figure *of* apocalypse, casting his cold yet participant eye on the horsemen who pass by, gazing with his 'kindly detachment, in farewell-detachment, in earth-departure-objectivity' (p. 108), almost extra-territorially, at the proposed departure from earth, seeing beyond it not only space but the final departure, which is death.

Clearly one resolution of his own perception is pure irony or disgust, and that is deeply present; but he too still has a journey, a need to decide between disgust and compassion. He lives now under the patronage of his physician nephew in the modern dereliction of late-sixties New York City, the biggest city on earth, surrounded by relatives and abundant street crowds who wander in assertion and violence preying strangely on each other, apparently drawn by the gravitational pull of some madness that makes them abuse both their society and their planet. Here he suitably meets his own guru, a modern Wellsian in the figure of Dr Govinda Lal, a biologist who sees mankind on the edge of some large adjustment to moon existence, and who, like Bellow's earlier gurus, quaintly expresses the angles of certain required truths. Between them, Sammler and Lal turn *Mr Sammler's Planet* into a neo-expository text, a work of extraordinary detachments and tonalities, of cosmic questions and anxieties: the closest thing, one might say, that Bellow has come to science fiction, not only by virtue of his subject but also by virtue of its persistent utterance of social and historical ideas. The world surrounds, intrudes on, indeed directly swamps their debates; life mocks ideas. But we can see, in that complex imbalance of ideas and world, the issues Bellow is concerned with: is the death of the world the birth of a new evolutionary thrust in man, to take him onward and elsewhere, or is it a suicidal apocalypse? But, equally, are such larger thoughts about biology and history diversions from the here-and-now, the immediate places where individual lives are undertaken and where they daily function or cease?

Mr Sammler's Planet has been read largely as a work of social indignation, a radical revolt against the radical revolt of 1968; it needs a larger view. It is indeed a novel where the streets of New York are filled with mad self-mythologizers, rampant with the assertion of self ('They legendize. They expand by imagination and try to rise above the limitations of the ordinary forms of common life', Sammler reflects (p. 118) in mixed fascination and outrage); it is populous with those modernized dandies who draw on that smell of liberal decay which dominates the novel, to seek ego-sainthood through a kind of madness. This sense of a dangerous new psycho-self emerging in culture haunts Bellow's later work; and certainly an explicit, fascinated, sexually troubled disgust, which would turn in his next novel toward a comic perception, runs through the book. Hence we could reasonably read it as emanating not only from the ironic survivor Sammler, but from the author, whose complex surrogate he undoubtedly is. Yet at the same time he is a clearly angled surrogate, whose ideas and whose voice should surely not be read as those of the author direct. The rapid chill economy of the novel's first paragraph both states but also tersely distances and abstractifies certain familiar Bellovian preoccupations ('The soul wanted what it wanted. It had its own natural knowledge. It sat unhappily on superstructures of explanation, poor bird, not knowing which way to fly' (p. 5)). The voice is willed, and has something of Dr Braun's irony and loss inside it, calling for restoration. The bleak vision of 'Millions of civilized people wanted oceanic, boundless, primitive, neckfree nobility, experienced a strange release of galloping impulses, and acquired the peculiar aim of sexual niggerhood for everyone' (p. 130) is measured against his recognition that, as his beloved Schopenhauer said, the Cosmic Will that transcends ideas has its seat in the sexual organs. Irony is turned as a force against the farce of the world by Sammler, a Gulliver returned from the land of Houyhnhnms to a debased place; but it is also turned against Sammler as, trying to 'live with a civil heart. With disinterested charity. With a sense of the mystic potency of mankind' (p. 110), he finds it hard to summon up most of these attributes, and longs to leave the planet to its fate.

Mr Sammler's Planet is again a book in a new voice; it is best read as a satirical novel, a work of detachment where disgust at the perversion of reason and feeling prevails. Yet Sammler, the voice of cosmic as well as recent human history, does have his own bleak lessons to learn as well as give. He has a sense of lapidary infinitude and of human and inhuman time, of the systems and causalities of modern despair. He sees that the power of irrationality is matched with the advance of mechanism, and that both function in a blameless state of madness, excluding the concentration of the full soul upon eternal being; that state of eternal being, his upward motion, is his primary concern. Yet there is an assignment for him, the refinement of the ethical imperative. *Mr Sammler's Planet* is a Swiftian text that reaches Platonically beyond the cave to transcendent knowledge, the real reality; but the reality is finally to be observed in its own human place. For *Mr Sammler's Planet*, like *Seize the Day*, ends before the deathbed of another, as Sammler gazes on Elya Gruner's corpse and sees in his greater corruption yet also his greater kindness an assertion of the necessary human contact which all must meet, because 'we know, we know, we know'.

5

THE 'IT' AND THE 'WE': 'HUMBOLDT'S GIFT' AND 'THE DEAN'S DECEMBER'

Maybe America didn't need art and inner miracles. It had so many outer ones. The USA was a big operation, very big. The more *it*, the less *we*. So Humboldt behaved like an eccentric and a comic subject. But occasionally there was a break in the eccentricity when he stopped and thought. He tried to think himself clear away from this American world (I did that, too). (*Humboldt's Gift*)

Mr Sammler's Planet, Bellow's bleak book for the end of the sixties, was not only Bellow's most apocalyptic but his most obviously pessimistic work – a work of sharp irony that played doubt alike over the specific conditions of modern culture, or post-culture, and the intensifying difficulties of discerning the contract underlying human existence. Its apparent tone of outrage and detachment dismayed a number of Bellow's critics, who, often missing its comic use of the innocent sexless stranger, felt in it both a waning of imaginative power and an angry conservative withdrawal from liberal humanism. It certainly marked another shift in the manner of his work, the signalling of a late Bellovian theme that was to develop further through the next two books, *Humboldt's Gift* (1975) and *The Dean's December* (1982), to date his newest novel. Bellow's work had always been shaped by concern with the states of modern history and the condition of modern consciousness – consciousness formed, as he puts it in *The Dean's December*, by the Hegelian understanding that tells us that the spirit of our time must be in us by nature. That spirit, and the suspicion that as a historical presence it is in a condition of extreme distortion, had always affected his characters. But now it was to become his work's central business to probe it – in the face of the possibility that, in that liberated post-romantic self which America models for us, there is secreted an obscenity, a new barbarism and decadence, which we take for a historical inevitability, yet which defeats any hope of our discovering a truly felt human nature. If *Mr Sammler's Planet* raises the question of the state of late twentieth-century civilization, its fall into its own underside, its toppling into a new grotesquerie and monstrosity, then the two following novels sustain the theme – though characteristically they search out new modes of writing about it, new speculations about how it might be apprehended.

It thus seems reasonable enough to read the vision of Bellow's later books as meditative commentaries on the earlier ones – the work of a writer who knows the essentiality of his own themes, but sees the task of their pursuit as open to endless self-questioning and refiguration, a refiguration itself conditioned by history and our changing maps of consciousness. Bellow's late books go on from *Mr Sammler's Planet* in being, above all, an enquiry or a kind of a culture-probe into a new American age: an age of mass, post-cultural energy, romantic expectation, of new élites and underclasses, of cities riven by exploited power and deprived crime, of energy and barbarism working side by side to the point where the implicated mind can find no way to question it – since the violence becomes an understandable phenomenon arising from the deprivation, the undersystem of the system above, and since we are historically contracted to it, older cultural bearings having been swept away. The age is indeed Lenin's age of 'wars and revolutions', when force rules and images of the end of the person abound; these later novels look for a new man of feeling who, seeking to reconcile the historical world with the larger powers of being, might by self-questioning encounter, without illusion or evasion, our fundamental nature. Bellow's novels now not only challenge apocalyptics, but also touch on their appropriateness, the need for what is called in *The Dean's December* 'catastrophe exposure'. Yet the problem is that explanations themselves obscure and contribute; just as politics and liberal reconciliations hide the crimes that are the products of damaged and depleted souls in a new age of monstrosity, so it is the larger soul beyond explanation that must be understood. To find a measurable position of detachment becomes the problem, both the necessity and the flaw; this indeed, in two quite different manners, is the theme of the two novels following on from *Mr Sammler's Planet*.

*

After the ironies of *Mr Sammler's Planet*, *Humboldt's Gift* appeared to many of Bellow's readers a text of surprise. It was a work not of hard irony but of comedy; in many ways it returned to the panoramic, picaresque, ebullient vein of the novels of the 1950s, while drawing, too, on the more intellectually centred action of the novels of the 1960s, with their comedy of swamping mental excess. Yet the new novel seemed to secrete within itself a commentary on Bellow's development up to this point – for one of its essential themes was the fate of the writer in different stages of modern American cultural development. A novel of oblique contracts, strange inheritances and dependencies, its story deals with two writers who represent two different literary-historical generations, and two different versions of cultural action. It is a novel of ways of addressing history, of two types of the creative individual attempting to respond to contemporary conditions and processes.[17] The older of the two is Von Humboldt Fleisher, poet and master-talker, 'a great entertainer but going insane'; he is cast as a writer in very much the 1950s spirit, a figure from the great *Partisan Review* age (Bellow has told us he is part modelled on his old friend Delmore Schwartz), when mass society appeared to need flamboyant intellectual saviours, Fisher Kings to interpret and in their own desperation to redeem the waste land. The younger is the book's narrator, Charlie Citrine, a latter-day survivor; now a successful novelist, he writes in a world where 'culture' seems furiously abundant but strangely compromised, caught up with money and power, violences and abuses, where there is indeed a new and unstable balance between financial and experiental abundance and the capacity to imagine, digest and interpret it, a dislocation between the 'it' and the 'we'.

In the book itself and in interviews at the time of its publication, Bellow emphasized this difference, identifying Humboldt as the 'early modernist' writer and Charlie Citrine as the author in a lowered season, making a 'comic end run'. That last phrase could easily be attached to Bellow's own tone and style in the book, the comedy of a high-minded survivor. Humboldt is a man of capitalized nouns who seeks to be a World Historical Individual, who lives a Success and dies a Failure, early, mad and poor; the problem he poses is that of how to define Art and Poetry in the modern world. Charlie, bound to him by curious intimacies, hostilities and contracts, is a writer of contingencies rather than grand abstractions; yet, confused amid a difficult divorce, an anxious love life, a deep awareness of the chaos of contemporary disorders, the irresolvable split between the world of the painted veil and the Platonic forms and the specifics and inadequacies of daily life, he does comically survive. Humboldt belongs to the more spectacular intellectual world of New York; Charlie chooses to return to Chicago, the dominant city of these two late books, a city of substantive materialism, mass, modernization, change, money, power, crime, where the great ideas have thinned enough to be seen through. He has grown used to the gap between the painted veils of eternity and the big money – the large income from his books which, he says, capitalism has given him for dark comical reasons of its own. Caught amid many contending versions of history, and the different ways in which the writer might come to feeling and understanding among them, Charlie's writing is there but his quest has really not yet begun.

It does so in the novel, where the multiple contracts in which Charlie has become engaged now have to be paid off. So, in the course of the book, Charlie is dragged through the law courts by divorce lawyers, invited to examine the nature of his emotional contracts with the past, forced to part with his money by the con-men, the entrepreneurs and men of power and violence, the mafiosi and the sexual partners with whom he has conducted his contingent relations, and finally forced to come to terms with the oblique contract he has with the dead, above all with Humboldt himself. Philip Roth once aptly noted – in *My Life as a Man* (1974) – that alimony battles had raged through America's courtrooms over the last decade 'the way religious wars raged through Europe in the seventeenth century', exposing marriage as a cash institution; in one sense or another, nearly all Charlie's relations turn out to be cash-nexus relations. For not only divorce court artists but many others pick Charlie's pockets – among them a not too successful racketeer named Rinaldo Cantabile, a *machismo* figure whose wife proves to be working on a PhD on Humboldt himself, and a well-breasted mistress named Renata (Citrine is contemporary enough to wish to sustain a high gratification threshold) who dumps her mother and child in his care in Spain, while she takes off to marry 'a serious man', an entrepreneurial funeral director. Art and money, sex and death, above all the tension between the modern world of the cash-and-culture nexus and that of the Platonic universals to which art traditionally is supposed to relate, are the dominant themes of the novel.

Money being the world's money, Charlie in fact loses it with some sense of great Chicago adventure, experiencing some virtue in the divestment, some proof of his transcendent concerns. But these present disturbances bring back his past, above all his relation to Humboldt, the poet to whom Charlie as a young man has gone as protégé, and whose attempt to reconcile the massiveness of the American universe with the Platonic functions of the imagination is his essential challenge. Humboldt, who has sought to link everything, Verlaine to the *Police Gazette*, the World Historical Individual to Harry Houdini (with whom Humboldt shares a birthplace in Appleton, Wisconsin), has in his time been massive and successful, acclaimed as a major American poet; he has also come to feel that culture is indeed rising in America, that imagination might wield political power, that he might take his own place in the political or the academic world, in a much-desired American synthesis. But this all collapses, as he slips into paranoia, madness, death in a flophouse; afterwards, however, he becomes famous for the success of his failure, making it 'in American Culture as Hart Schaffner & Marx made it in cloaks and suits . . . he died and got good notices' (*HG*, pp. 118, 120). It is just around the time of Humboldt's death that Charlie has his success, consorting with the Kennedys, pushed by an ambitious wife who would make JFK 'an excellent Secretary of State, if some way could be found to wake her before 11 a.m.' (p. 59). But Humboldt's vision of a happy relation between art and power has long since gone; Charlie now has to live, without the ambitious wife, though with her high alimony expectations, in a new America, an age of the wised-up rabble, where society rewards and demolishes its artists indiscriminately, by making art affluent succour, by swathing itself in cultural goods, by joking with the imagination while denying its lessons.

'What we had in Chicago', Charlie notes, 'was a cultureless city pervaded nevertheless by Mind' (p. 70). Developing from the early great novelists of the windy city, Frank Norris, Theodore Dreiser and Upton Sinclair, who presented Chicago as a bustling commercial metropolis where culture is passed to women or the idle, or is simply dislocated by the material, Bellow extends the enquiry to create a new image, reversing the old accusation to depict a new, and typically modern, unstable mixture. Here it is apt for the wife of a mafioso to be working on a PhD in literature; here 'Policemen take psychology courses and have some feeling for the comedy of urban life' (p. 53). Sammler had seen New York as a city of 'hypercivilized Byzantine luxury' (*MSP*, p. 8); Chicago extends the problem, becoming a comic but cannibal world of crime and power, violent sensibilities and incomprehensible tolerances, crude concepts and fashionable styles, of flamboyant selfhood and civil void, boom and boredom. Bellow's dense Chicago embraces the Playboy Club and the old Russian baths in the devastated ghetto, the muggers and sudden deaths in the buses, and hanging in the air the old death smell of the stockyards that persists long after their disappearance. It is the new opulent city that dominates, and Bellow makes it exemplary of a new America, where a new comic demonology of crime and power, of changed relations ('History had created something new in the USA, namely crookedness with self-respect or duplicity with honour' (*HG*, p. 217)), requires something new of the contemporary artist; for all his 'other-wordliness', Charlie consorts with a new era of gangsters and hooligans, opportunists and men of fashion and power, speculators in profit who are simultaneously speculators in his own product, which is Mind.

Thus culture and corruption are bound together in some energetic and challenging new relationship; of them Bellow creates an extraordinary modern gallery, of wild wives, entrepreneurial intellectuals, men of dubious but real power, ex-actors who are construction men, fences who are men of taste. In Renata, 'the carnal artist', Citrine himself acquires a risky symbol of Platonic beauty, a strange place to reconcile his mental and his erotic life; he forms an equally strange alliance to Cantabile, who has smashed Citrine's Mercedes to recover a gambling debt and then draws him into a strange alliance of artist and con-man, for gangsterism has grown respectable, and art become hungry for the underworld of violence, for a 'greater intensity'. Boredom and terror are the motors of modern life: men drive themselves to heart attacks playing racquet ball at the club, rich sexual gratifications of every kind are on offer; the style artists gather together and a new post-culture spawns. On this boredom itself Charlie becomes a specialist, reflecting that this is a world where 'nothing actual ever suits pure expectation and such purity of expectation is a great source of tedium' (p. 196).

Humboldt's Gift is thus an enormous, sprawling, intensely comic novel about the problems of the creative self in a new world of mind, a world not of history but of versions of history, not of psyche but of versions of psyches. Outward reality is indeed so vast and so fanciful that it seems of no use to try to make sense of an inner one; yet Charlie feels a certain need to

89

leave Tolstoy's 'false and unnecessary comedy of history' (*HG*, p. 464) and simply begin to live. Charlie, Bellow's late-life quester, indeed tries, seeking for a vigorous tug from the realm of the mystical and the Platonic, turning for reassurance to the works of Rudolph Steiner, insisting that 'the soul belongs to a greater, an all-embracing life outside. It's got to' (p. 324). He pursues his search for his 'early and peculiar sense of existence. . . . I was quite a nut about such things' (p. 6), finding, however, that society, which 'trains you in distraction', is not fully to be left.

As with most of Bellow's heroes, the attempt to make the imagination and the self transcendent is not totally achieved. Charlie may have learned from Tolstoy that 'It's time we simply refused to be inside history and playing the comedy of history, the bad social game' (p. 124), but he also recognizes that real life is a relation between here and there. The lawsuits, fiscal contracts and sexual transactions are one thing; there may be a higher rate of exchange. For signs of the promise, he has, like all Bellow's later heroes, hints from an older Jewish past, though these too are compromised – the Russian baths of Chicago survive amid the ruins, but are now probably owned by gangsters; the Platonic self and the carnal self never quite mesh. Citrine's Platonic glimpses seem to point to the terms of the ultimate contract, opening up that 'star world within us that can be seen when the spirit takes a new vantage point outside the body' (p. 384) and points to a communion of souls; but he indeed observes that 'The painted veil isn't what it used to be' (p. 20) and his task in any case is to be the appropriate artist of this deeply changed world.

Thus it is that Humboldt leaves him several gifts. Attempting to master everything, from Verlaine to the *Police Gazette*, and to write the artist large in the modern world, he has failed to reconcile art and power and dies in a flophouse. Of him Citrine observes: 'the radiance he dealt with was the old radiance and it was in short supply. What was needed was a new radiance altogether' (p. 107). Citrine, moved to Chicago and caught in a yet more massive contingency, has attempted to survive in the space Humboldt has left behind; the story is of his finding a new space which is a communion with the dead. For death is another of Humboldt's inheritances, a death that does not stay the same but itself has to be modernized; at the end of the novel Citrine awards him an expensive modern burial in a latter-day mechanical mausoleum, where a 'condensation of collective intelligence and combined ingenuities, its cables silently spinning, dealt with the individual poet' (p. 474).

It is one of Bellow's more muted and comic final burials, an oblique transcendental contract, an oblique recovery. Humboldt is modernized, and Charlie contracted to him, in other ways too, most notably through the specific gift Humboldt passes across the grave in the form of a film script, which not only speculates on the theme of cannibalism and repentance, but restores Charlie's financial fortunes. But above all Charlie inherits the new version of Humboldt's task, which he had once described as attempting to fit 'queer American bodies . . . into art's garments' (p. 334); the legacy is to find the modern form of art. Bellow finds it in late modern comedy: Charlie endures, survives and enlarges, as does his creator, making his own comic end run in the form of, not a high modernist text, but a text in and about history, modern contingency and chaos, contemporary consciousness in its boredom, terror and turbulence. This is a novel about transcendence and history, and about the style through which the novelist might give us both by working between social contingency and absurdity and the curious eternal power of the imaginative act, presented as neither modernist in its formal wholeness, nor post-modernist in its fundamental self-doubt, but in the novel as conditional form.

*

A year after the publication of *Humboldt's Gift* Bellow won the Nobel Prize and spoke of the need to move on in his work, and to write of people who make a more spirited resistance to the forces of our time. In the event, seven years passed before a new novel, *The Dean's December* (1982), appeared – though in the interim Bellow published a work of non-fiction, *To*

Jerusalem and Back: A Personal Account (1976), which is both an intense personal memoir and a deeply pro-Israeli work. *The Dean's December* seemed less a spectacular move on than a solemn move back over Bellow's understandings and lasting concerns, a deeply serious late book that, with a new weight rather than a new form, circled like a mediation over the previous ground. Bellow's books from *Herzog* on had concerned themselves with measuring the state of a new world order, with the models of being that serve to state our places in it, with the overwhelming past of ideas and the overwhelming presentness of their consequences. In *Mr Sammler's Planet* ironically, in *Humboldt's Gift* comically, the scale of Bellow's late enterprise becomes apparent, as he seeks to penetrate and find the heroes and the forms for a world that has lost its old cultural bearings, broken with its past, moved into some new and apocalyptic condition of historical being where boredom and terror, crime and indifference, dark new underclasses and a new topside anarchy of Byzantine wealth and chaotic power co-exist; Charlie Citrine's underlying horror, as he contemplates the new boredom, is that 'If there are only foolish minds and mindless bodies there'll be nothing serious to annihilate. In the highest government positions almost no human beings have been seen for decades now, anywhere in the world', so that 'Mankind must recover its imaginative powers, recover living thought and real being, no longer accept these insults to its soul, and do it soon' (*HG*, p. 245). These may be read as fundamental modern themes, and to Bellow they impose a special urgency on the arts, the place of those 'imaginative powers'; at the same time Bellow's tone in these matters has been found, by some of his readers, conservative, socially secured. In fact Bellow's characteristic tone has always been complex, a mixture of engaged imaginative investment in this perceived history and a critical withdrawal; but a certain sense of victimization and a more articulate need to justify and also to question this theme clearly haunts *The Dean's December*, perhaps his most considered book.

The Dean's December is a novel close to meditation or

self-dialogue, and a book generally as solemn as its main setting, contemporary communist Bucharest, a city with a 'livid death moment' in its air as the night comes up. It is in fact a 'Tale of Two Cities'; against Bucharest, remarkably evoked in its institutional life, there is again Chicago, a city seen in its 'wounds, lesions, cancers, destructive fury, death' (*DD*, p. 201) though also, like Bucharest, in its forms of personal life. The problem Bellow seems directly to pose is how we write an adequate account of our perceptions, and find our state of being, in a world that is so pressing as to make any system of explanation suspect, for modern life is run with systems of explanation, concepts.

In *The Dean's December*, Bellow explores a new hero, a new man of feeling, who, like Sammler and Citrine, knows his own complicity, is in some ways shamed by his own self-questioning, yet who still has some need to encounter his own fundamental human nature, to discover the place of the true soul which feels. He is Albert Corde, a former journalist who has reported large political events, but has stepped back from these by becoming a Professor of Journalism, and a Dean, at a Chicago university, thereby hoping to recover the world of ideas, of poetry, of adequate critical observation. At the same time he is a man of ordinary affairs ('Face it, the cosmos was beyond him' (p. 14)), in contrast to his Romanian-born wife Minna, educated by her communist mother to escape from the containments and pressures of political life by turning to science. She has come to America and is an astro-physicist ('She did boundless space, his beat was terra firma' (p. 261)).

But both Corde and Minna are tugged back into the historical world by two events. In Chicago, Corde discloses himself in two magazine articles for *Harper's* on the topic of Chicago – the great new shining upstart metropolis, where both the big new skyscrapers and the crime rates rise over derelict lots, entire vandalized districts, a displaced and violent underclass, where the bourgeois doors that protect the Byzantine, therapeutic topside life are triple-locked, and the city cuts beneath itself a great hundred-mile-long sewer into which its skyscrapers might tip. Corde's articles reflect on the crimes, corruptions and liberal inertias; on the prisons, hospitals, violences and abuses of the city, in what Corde sees as an impassioned detachment, an analytic but also an apocalyptic dismay. These opinions make him unpopular among friends and colleagues. Then one of the students for whom he is responsible, as Dean, is murdered in a complex and senseless crime, with sexual and racial overtones. Corde pushes for an investigation and a conviction and members of his own family become his adversaries, in the courtroom and outside it, once two streetwise blacks have been charged with the murder.

In Bucharest, Minna's mother, a former Minister of Health, once purged, now part-rehabilitated, is dying; they fly to the bedside, only to discover that she is in a governmental institution where her contacts with others are being manipulated, so that they find themselves blocked by the authorities from seeing her regularly. Bucharest is the book's main setting, with the Chicago story unfolding in the distance, as Corde, imprisoned in the family apartment in a hostile city, reflects on past events and receives news and some friends from home; the two cities interlock into versions of the modern world, each generating dismay.

As in Bellow's earlier novels, if with a new solemnity, it is death that dominates the novel: the anarchic murder of the Chicago student, the politically manipulated mortality of Valeria, and then the events of her funeral. The Chicago story is, like *Humboldt's Gift*, dominated by litigations, accusations, lawyers, courtrooms; and Corde's main adversary is his young nephew Mason, who has identified with 'the youth racket' and the streetwise blacks he believes to be victimized in the necessary way of life they have made. The Bucharest story is dominated by the powerfully institutionalized system of surveillance, the functioning of a politics of pain; here Corde's main adversary is a KGB colonel responsible for the hospital, one of the old generation who is determined to challenge not only Minna's act of defection but also Corde's political innocence and his western decadence. In Chicago, there are 'whirl-

94

ing souls', living a febrile life either of deprivation or of influence and comforts in 'the modern consciousness, the queer equivocal condition' (p. 130); in Bucharest, Corde knows himself as 'the image of the inappropriate American – in all circumstances inappropriate, incapable of learning the lessons of the twentieth century; spared, or scorned, by the forces of history or fate or whatever a European might want to call them' (p. 3).

As the two deaths interlock, being both historical and political, the outcome of two modern conditions of man, so too do the two essential stories of the novel and the balance they create between two primary versions of modern social order – the totalitarian system, where power and force are exerted against individuals, but where the traces of the old order still show in the dignified personal relations of domestic life; the pleasure-principle order of America, where a different kind of harness and toughness serve on the streets and in the practice of power, where the past is razed and an unfurnished meagre modern consciousness thrives.

Corde, the man of feeling with all this to reconcile, is appropriately one of Bellow's most muted heroes. His attempt to discover an appropriate angry detachment, to find a journalistic poetry to 'recover the world that is buried under the debris of false description or nonexperience' (p. 243) and to penetrate beyond concepts, is threatened as he moves, in Bucharest, through the bleak official world of cremation and burial following Valeria's death. He goes from the heated depths of the crematorium, where the corpses are ridden toward the incinerator, to the cold surrealist graveyard where the mourners gather around the tomb that is the wrong shape to admit the box of ashes.

Beyond the fundamental Bellovian encounter with mortality and its temporal meanings, there are the questions of appropriate emotion and explanation – the failure, for example, of his own historical concepts to explain to Minna the conflicting and part-hostile emotion she feels toward her mother after her death; the failure, probed by a journalist friend, Dewey Spangler, to think exactly and without excessive poetry or apocalyptics about the first and last things. Likewise the novel seems to end on an equally tentative balance, as Corde, still seeking for the soul that apprehends beyond appearances in historical time, loses his academic post and accompanies Minna to the Mount Palomar observatory. Here he rises up in the elevator of the telescope toward the cold of the universe, defeated in his hopes of discovering an appropriately academic detachment but drawn to attend to what had been neglected, the marks of the heavens, distorted by atmosphere, through which are seen

> objects, forms, partial realities. The rest was to be felt. And it wasn't only that you felt, but that you were drawn to feel and to penetrate further, as if you were being informed that what was spread over you had to do with your existence, down to the very blood and the crustal forms inside your bones. Rocks, trees, animals, men and women, these also drew you to penetrate further, under the distortions (comparable to the atmospheric ones, shadows within shadows), to find their real being with your own. That was the sense in which you were being drawn. (p. 311)

The theme is not new, but the tone is: a view from an intense historical seriousness into what our place in the larger cosmos might mean in the discovery of adequate feeling.

6

'A NIGHTMARE DURING WHICH I'M TRYING TO GET A GOOD NIGHT'S REST': CONCLUSION

He had read many thousands of books. He said that history was a nightmare during which he was trying to get a good night's rest. Insomnia made him more learned. In the small hours he read thick books — Marx and Sombart, Toynbee, Rostovzeff, Freud . . . (*Humboldt's Gift*)

In 1953, in *Partisan Review*, the magazine where Bellow began his writing career, one of the editors, Philip Rahv, published an article, 'The Myth and the Powerhouse', which reflected on contemporary 'mythomania' — for this was the high season of American myth-criticism. For many post-war critics, he said, 'the supertemporality of myth provides the ideal refuge from history', adding that 'To the mythmakers as to Stephen Dedalus in *Ulysses* history is a nightmare from which they are trying to awake. But to awake from history into myth is like escaping from a nightmare into a state of permanent insomnia.'[18] It is not far-fetched to suppose that when Bellow, at the opening of *Humboldt's Gift*, evokes the great mental and literary resources of Humboldt, 'the Mozart of gab', emphasizes his insomnia and has him speak of history as 'a nightmare during which he was trying to get a good night's rest', he is recalling Rahv and that much-discussed tension between the imaginative myths of fiction and the commanding powerhouse of historical process. Humboldt is one of Bellow's modern intellectual heroes, one of those who lives in the post-Romantic inheritance, in Augie March's turbulent abundance of ideas too big to hold, Herzog's massive thought accumulation, so comically great that it forbids feeling and reflection. And the joke about *Ulysses* invites us to consider the response one essential strand of modernism offered to the nightmare of history – the move to spatial-symbolist form, the shift from contingently historiographical fiction toward fiction as myth or myth-parody (so with *Ulysses* Homer's long myth-epic of a nation's founding and a wanderer's return becomes an epic of consciousness and Dublin, held within the unhistorical cycle of a single day). It was because modernist writing seemed to encourage mythic interpretations and the avoidance of historical awareness in the post-political mood of the 1950s that Rahv urged the necessary reminder that the Nietzschean sixth sense, that of historicism, was essential if the imagination was to grasp the world and not simply see it as senseless change.

Rahv's challenge was relevant because American thought has often been disposed to see history as a 'European' phenomenon – a point Bellow makes in several of his novels, including *The Dean's December*. Certainly the drive toward the mythic mode has always been powerful in American writing – as if this was the necessary counterforce to history's 'absence'. Yet that apparent absence has equally been a powerful theme *within* American writing; the presenting of historiography in American fiction has been far more evident than the myth-oriented critics have stressed. James Fenimore Cooper's Leatherstocking may be, as R. W. B. Lewis argues in *The American Adam* (1955), a 'hero in space', romantically transcendent and removed from historical time; but Cooper always carefully explores his place in the evolving historical process of settlement and rising civilization in America. Hawthorne's *The House of the Seven Gables* (1851) may be a 'romance', but it is also a pointed fable of history in process and change; process is the name of the train that carries Clifford and Hepzibah from their old social retreat into modern secular democratic solitude, just as it is the force that shifts Melville's Billy Budd (*Billy Budd, Sailor*, posthumous, 1924) from the eighteenth-century pastoral world to the new industrial city of the nineteenth-century warship.

Seeking the timeless symbol, the great nineteenth-century American writers also set it against the commanding historical process. With naturalism, American fiction found names and scientific explanations for those forcefields that were set in and against the lives of individuals: biological theories of heredity, sociological theories of environment, historical theories of change and evolution, of incremental energy, exponential growth, what Henry Adams called the modern 'multiverse'. Many of the great works of American modernism, from William Faulkner's *The Sound and the Fury* (1929) to John Dos Passos's *USA* (1936), are structured according to both historical-evolutionary and spatial-symbolic principles. For Scott Fitzgerald, Freud spoke of consciousness and Marx of history; his later work was an attempt to reconcile these two forces and so come to terms with the secular clock which functions within modern consciousness.

It is my point that, despite the myth-critics, the problem of relating history to consciousness and style has always been a fundamental preoccupation of the American novel. And, despite the insistence on the fictionality of much contemporary experimental American fiction, this has been true in post-war fiction too: in Mailer and Roth, in Vonnegut and Pynchon. The sense of a historical lesion, often focused in the tragic events of the Second World War and reinforced by modern technological and cybernetic materialism, intensifies the problems of representing consciousness and finding fictional form; hence we seem to move toward a post-humanist novel. In a world where Freud and Marx call for synthesis, and the answer seems to be therapeutic models of the self, the expression of new Byzantine selfhoods, stylish performances of the ego that at once assert their historical alertness and their freedom from any conditions of history, where people hence behave 'as if they come from another place, another life, and that they have inpulses and desires that nothing in the world, none of our present premises, can account for' (*HG*, p. 467), the modern writer is forced to be attentive to a world of subjective revolutions and flamboyant lifestyles which at once assert and reject

99

an idea of historical reality. In his book *The Triumph of the Therapeutic* (1966), Philip Rieff explores a model of post-cultural culture in which a cognate relation between interior understanding and the institutions of society disappears. A liberal-therapeutic model of the self takes its place, giving us a world of contemporaneity as parody, a world of polyglot goods and chattels, therapeutic self-discoveries exhausted quickly, life passages and wayward desires ritualized as human growth, the Romantic revolution rewarded.

Bellow, it seems to me, is and has always been the novelist as the creative explorer and invigilator of such a world, a world of historical, material and psychological abundance, an era of the Niagara Falls of history and culture, under which the self seems both aggrandized and dwarfed. Today we are surrounded, suggests Bellow, not just by History but by thoughts about History, versions of liberation and anomie, images of entitlement and plight, ideas drawn from both nineteenth-century positivism and twentieth-century irrationalism. Images of violence are turned into benefit, ideas of excess turned into health, cultures of superfluity turned into need. Crime and power consort together, hiding the evidence of barbarism; monstrosity becomes understandable and therefore self-sufficient. Bellow is a novelist conspicuously learned in those ideas, their development, their outcome and their consequences: 'Any philosopher who wants to keep his contact with mankind should pervert his own system in advance to see how it will really look a few decades after adoption,' Herzog writes to 'Dear Herr Nietzsche' (*H*, p. 327). Indeed many of his characters are conspicuously frenzied by them, in endless mental engagement and quarrel, and Bellow is that rare thing in modern American fiction, a genuinely intellectual novelist for whom the world of ideas is of the essence, yet who manages to be a bestseller. But if history, for Bellow, means this mental abundance, it also means conditions and processes; schooled, like his own characters, in Romanticism and behaviourism, in liberalism, empiricism and idealism, his task is the heuristic one to penetrate the fictions of reality that surround us and at the

100

same time to find the means for discovering and expressing his own sense of a reality beyond the fictions.

Bellow's work is thus shaped by the knowledge that process and environment are determining powers over man, as he shows us in *The Victim*, but that degrees of freedom are possible and we can forge a character that can challenge our fate, as he suggests in *The Adventures of Augie March*. He recognizes that consciousness is a collective historical flow, and is bonded into us, as he shows us in *The Dean's December*; he at the same time proposes that the mind may remodel the offered versions of reality and its images of narcissism, as in *Herzog*. He identifies the power of the massive accumulated stock of concepts, the weight of the 'it' that dwarfs the 'we' in *Humboldt's Gift*; in the same book he sees a possible reversal, a process whereby ideas are conserved, redeemed as consciousness, as felt forms of existence, so that they are no longer ideas. Bellow is a historicist novelist in quarrel with history, to the degree that it immerses us, or justifies us; he refuses to see us as nothing more than historical causes or instances, and for this he requires that half-absurd but fundamentally necessary sense of numinism or symbolism possessed by his characters when they touch intensity, the time of the spacious universe, the infolded presence of life.

So, out of Bellow's rhythms of stress, his immersion in and quarrel with history, the characteristic Bellovian endings arise, where some transcendental illumination occurs, silence comes, life is seen in the view of death, self in the view of the other. A balanced sense of reality is sought; so is a transcendent composure. In this there is often a reinvigorated sense of civility or social membership, though in the later novels this is qualified if not forgone. The beginnings may start in the contentions of a felt and immediate history; the endings suggest composure following flux. But they are ambiguous, not alone because in one obvious sense, understood by Bellow, there is no way we may transcend history, but because they are themselves brief moments without a complete finality, because they have the rhetorical function of endings and because they are characteristically stepping stones toward a new novel in which we are returned, precisely, toward the beginning. The rhythm of Bellow's books is ceaseless, continuous and very much in history, a history of perverting culture and misled consciousness in which we exist inescapably but from which recoveries into the 'peculiar sense of existence' are still possible. And that history, of which Bellow has offered us ever more encompassing versions, itself endlessly puts the imagination to the test, challenges it, victimizes it, diminishes it as an authority.

It is not hard to see that Bellow's sense of history is both highly American – though his America is the outcome of the crucial thought-movements of Europe – and conservative, an increasingly indignant assault on a civilization in decay. The moralist can easily grow narrow in defending the terms of his moral insight (as, in fact, I think Bellow does in *To Jerusalem and Back*, where the moral sensitivities fail to encompass the sufferings of the new Arab diaspora); the educated novelist can grow detached in his perception of the 'new mental rabble of the wised-up world' (*HG*, p. 107); the writer from the warm ghetto can feel perhaps an excessive emptiness in the new city. Yet Bellow *is* a novelist of immersion, and he is a novelist of immense artistic authority, an authority drawn from the repeated rhythm of self-questioning that undercuts his own concepts and the process of conceptualization itself. Hence the fertility of Bellow's quarrel with the coercions of modern thought; and his determined investment in the imagination, the 'painted veil', in the development of his books and in his development from one book to another. Hence, too, his committed devotion to the idea of the self, the inner being ('I admit', says Charlie Citrine, 'this private sphere has become so repulsive that we are glad to get away from it' (*HG*, p. 245)).

It is bourgeois individualist man, we might say, that Bellow protects by his transcendentalism; yet in centring, liberally, on that essential essence the felt person, without which individuals become biological rubbish in the cosmic process or else political dross in the maps of history and power, Bellow equally challenges the romantic egomania, the modern psycho-buffoon who has not a life but a lifestyle, and who, as Sammler says, wears self as an ornament which looks from the outside like a millstone. Bellow's preserved act of the imagination and his sense of what constitutes the felt presence of self are entirely consistent; it is for this reason that his novels are formally authoritative without being experimental.

All these are Bellow's abiding quarrels and stresses, his rhythms and preoccupations. But if we want a word that proposes the nature of his response and suggests his essential form, then that word is surely 'comedy'. As early as *Dangling Man*, Joseph had perceived comedy as the one power the self possesses; there is, he reflects, an 'element of the comic or fantastic in everyone' which cannot be brought under control. In that element of the comic or fantastic lies the sense of our potency and our distinctiveness, our sense that against the 'it' there is indeed a 'we'. It is expressed as a sense of man's absurd exposure in *Dangling Man*, as a mysterious metaphysics of connection in *The Victim*, as a euphoric mode of self-discovery in *The Adventures of Augie March*, as a fantastic intercourse with the world of nature in *Henderson the Rain King*. It is a self-compensating madness in *Herzog*, an ironic mode of survival in *Mr Sammler's Planet*, an eccentric legacy in *Humboldt's Gift*, a metaphorical connection between terra firma and the cosmos in *The Dean's December*. It points toward the measuring of an adequate mean for man in a world that, according to most present offered logics of causality, offers none. It is a comedy of the mind in serious process, enjoying its own inventive splendours, recognizing its restrictions and acknowledging its insufficiencies. As fictional form, it is the text that refuses to contain itself within its own laws of formalism, but opens up to changing historical pressures in order to try to distil the changeable point at which the power of the imagination might be asserted.

Bellow remains one of our most serious novelists, and our most commanding, because he is a great modern novelist of the attempt to reconcile mind, in all its resource and confusion, its fantastic fertility and unending anguish, with a life that is itself

103

absurd, extravagant, pressing us not only with material forces but with ideas and forms of consciousness, information and concepts, boredoms and rewards. It is a world where the measure of man can hardly be taken, the right form of expression or idea never be found; but where our mind as a sense of felt existence insists that we take it. The resulting perception is indeed comedy in its seriousness: which is an observation of disparity, an awareness that we are, indeed, 'suffering jokers', vital but absurd, and of a secret freedom, lying in our gift to know. History, environment, concept and the reality-instructors tell us much, and much of it makes us despair; but against that there is a self-presence, vivid and curious, and of it Bellow is surely one of the great modern metaphysical comedians.

NOTES

1 Details are from Mark Schorer, *Sinclair Lewis: An American Life* (London: Heinemann, 1961), especially pp. 343–67; Harrison Smith (ed.), *From Main Street to Stockholm: Letters of Sinclair Lewis, 1919–1930* (New York: Harcourt Brace, 1952), pp. 262 –302; Joseph Blotner, *Faulkner: A Biography*, 2 vols (London: Chatto & Windus, 1974), especially pp. 1337–74; Carlos Baker, *Hemingway: A Life Story* (London: Collins, 1969), pp. 619–23; and Elaine Steinbeck and Robert Wallsten (eds), *Steinbeck: A Life in Letters* (London: Heinemann, 1975), pp. 742–64.

2 See interview with W. J. Weatherby, *The Guardian*, 10 November 1976.

3 Saul Bellow, 'The Nobel Lecture', *The American Scholar*, 46 (Summer 1977), pp. 16–25.

4 Leslie Fiedler, *Waiting for the End: The American Literary Scene from Hemingway to Baldwin* (London: Cape, 1965), p. 84.

5 Lionel Trilling, *The Liberal Imagination: Essays on Literature and Society* (New York: Viking Press, 1950). Trilling's work can be profitably read as essential intellectual background to Bellow, and charts parallel desires for a 'moral' fiction turned towards realism, as well as a conviction that the essential lesson of Freud is the struggle with irrational adversaries, the opposing self.

6 Morris Dickstein, *Gates of Eden: American Culture in the Sixties* (New York: Basic Books, 1977).

7 Nathan A. Scott, *Three American Moralists: Mailer, Bellow, Trilling* (Notre Dame, Ind.: University of Notre Dame Press, 1973), p. 105.

8 See Gordon L. Harper, 'Saul Bellow, The Art of Fiction: An Interview', *Paris Review*, 37 (Winter 1965), pp. 48–73; reprinted in Earl Rovit (ed.), *Saul Bellow: A Collection of Critical Essays* (Englewood Cliffs, NJ: Prentice-Hall, 1975), pp. 5–18.

9 Ihab Hassan, 'Saul Bellow: Five Faces of a Hero', *Critique*, 3 (Summer 1960). This issue contains useful essays and bibliography. Hassan's article is valuably extended in his *Radical Innocence: Studies in the Contemporary American Novel* (Princeton, NJ: Princeton University Press, 1961).

10 Saul Bellow, 'Some Notes on Recent American Fiction', *Encounter*, 21 (November 1963), pp. 22–9; reprinted in Malcolm Bradbury (ed.), *The Novel Today: Writers on Modern Fiction* (Manchester and London: Manchester University Press and Fontana, 1977), pp. 54–70. Also, Saul Bellow, 'Literature', in Mortimer Adler and Robert M. Hutchins (eds), *The Great Ideas Today* (Chicago, Ill.: Encyclopaedia Britannica, 1963), pp. 163–4. For Bellow's views of comedy and a reading of his comic methods see Sarah Blacher Cohen, *Saul Bellow's Enigmatic Laughter* (Urbana and Chicago, Ill., and London: University of Illinois Press, 1974).

11 'Introduction', in Saul Bellow (ed.), *Great Jewish Short Stories* (New York: Dell, 1963).

12 Quoted in Harper, op. cit.

13 Robert Scholes, *The Fabulators* (New York: Oxford University Press, 1967).

14 Judie Newman, in an unpublished lecture, has taken these points further, observing that Bellow always takes seriously Ortega y Gasset's dictum, quoted in *The Adventures of Augie March*, that 'Man has not a nature but a history', and that Henderson encounters fundamental models of history in Africa: the Arnewi live in a Golden Age timeless pastoral, the Wariri in a fallen cylical history, and Henderson has the American prophetic-progressive view; hence the 'supposedly "mythic" or "romance" setting is merely a pretext to an exploration of the very bases of the historical sense.'

15 In the valuable study K. M. Opdahl, *The Novels of Saul Bellow: An Introduction* (University Park, Pa, and London: Pennsylvania State University Press, 1967), Opdahl usefully emphasizes that when Henderson feels at last at home in the cold he has come to terms with the 'cosmic coldness' of death and inanimation which has haunted him through the book.

16 Quoted in Harper, op. cit.

17 There are valuable comments on this in Judie Newman, 'Saul Bellow: *Humboldt's Gift* – The Comedy of History', *Durham University Journal*, 72, 1 (December 1979), pp. 79–87.

18 Philip Rahv, 'The Myth and the Powerhouse', *Partisan Review* (1953); reprinted in Philip Rahv, *Literature and the Sixth Sense* (Boston Mass.: Houghton Mifflin, 1969), pp. 202–15.

BIBLIOGRAPHY

WORKS BY SAUL BELLOW

Novels

Dangling Man. New York: Vanguard, 1944. London: John Lehmann, 1946.

The Victim. New York: Vanguard, 1947. London: John Lehmann, 1948.

The Adventures of Augie March. New York: Viking Press, 1953. London: Weidenfeld & Nicolson, 1954.

Seize the Day. New York: Viking Press, 1956 (American edition includes 'A Father to Be', 'Looking for Mr Green', 'The Gonzaga Manuscripts' and *The Wrecker*). London: Weidenfeld & Nicolson, 1957.

Henderson the Rain King. New York: Viking Press, 1959. London: Weidenfeld & Nicolson, 1959.

Herzog. New York: Viking Press, 1964. London: Weidenfeld & Nicolson, 1965.

Mosby's Memoirs, and Other Stories. New York: Viking Press, 1968. London: Weidenfeld & Nicolson, 1969.

Mr Sammler's Planet. New York: Viking Press, 1970. London: Weidenfeld & Nicolson, 1970.

Humboldt's Gift. New York: Viking Press, 1975. London: Alison Press/Secker & Warburg, 1975.

The Dean's December. New York: Harper & Row, 1982. London: Alison Press/Secker & Warburg, 1982.

Play

The Last Analysis. New York: Viking Press, 1965.

Chief uncollected stories

'Two Morning Monologues'. *Partisan Review*, 8 (May–June 1941), pp. 230–6.

'The Mexican General'. *Partisan Review*, 9 (May–June 1942), pp. 178–94.

'A Sermon by Doctor Pep'. *Partisan Review*, 14 (May 1949), pp. 455–62.

'The Trip to Galena'. *Partisan Review*, 17 (November–December 1960), pp. 769–94.

'Address by Gooley MacDowell to the Hasbeens Club of Chicago'. *Hudson Review*, 4 (Summer 1951), pp. 222–7.

Main non-fiction

Translation of Isaac Bashevis Singer, 'Gimpel the Fool'. *Partisan Review*, 20 (May–June 1954), pp. 300–13.

'Distractions of a Fiction Writer'. In Granville Hicks (ed.), *The Living Novel*. New York: Macmillan, 1957.

'The Writer As Moralist'. *Atlantic Monthly*, 221 (March 1963), pp. 58–62.

'Literature'. In Morton Adler and Robert M. Hutchins (eds), *Great Ideas Today*. Chicago, Ill.: Encyclopaedia Britannica, 1963.

'Introduction'. In Saul Bellow (ed.), *Great Jewish Short Stories*. New York: Dell, 1963.

To Jerusalem and Back: A Personal Account. New York: Viking Press, 1976. London: Alison Press/Secker & Warburg, 1976.

'Some Notes on Recent American Fiction'. *Encounter*, 21 (November 1963), pp. 22–9. Reprinted in M. Bradbury (ed.), *The Novel Today: Writers on Modern Fiction*. Manchester and London: Manchester University Press and Fontana, 1977. Totowa, NJ: Rowman & Littlefield, 1977.

'The Nobel Lecture'. Reprinted in *The American Scholar*, 46 (Summer 1977), pp. 16–25.

BIBLIOGRAPHY

Lercangée, Francine. *Saul Bellow: A Bibliography of Secondary Sources*. Brussels: Centre for American Studies, 1977.

Nault, Marianne. *Saul Bellow: His Works and His Critics: An Annotated International Bibliography*. London: Garland, 1977.

Nevius, Blake. *The American Novel: Sinclair Lewis to the Present*. New York: Appleton-Century-Crofts, 1970.

Noreen, Robert G. *Saul Bellow: A Reference Guide*. Boston, Mass.: G. K. Hall, 1978.

For bibliographical material and critical articles, see also *The Saul Bellow Newsletter* (Department of English, Wayne State University, Detroit, Michigan).

SELECTED CRITICISM OF SAUL BELLOW

Baumbach, Jonathan. *The Landscape of Nightmare*. New York: New York University Press, 1965. London: Peter Owen, 1966.

Clayton, John J. *Saul Bellow: In Defense of Man*. Bloomington, Ind.: Indiana University Press, 1968. 2nd edn 1979.

Cohen, Sara B. *Saul Bellow's Enigmatic Laughter*. Urbana and Chicago, Ill., and London: University of Illinois Press, 1974.

Critique, 7 (Spring–Summer 1965). Saul Bellow Special Number.

Dommergues, Pierre. *Saul Bellow*. Paris: Grasset, 1967.

Dutton, Robert R. *Saul Bellow*. New York: Twayne, 1971.

Eisinger, Chester E. *Fiction of the Forties*. Chicago, Ill., and London: University of Chicago Press, 1963.

Galloway, David D. 'The Absurd Man as Picaro: The Novels of Saul Bellow'. *Texas Studies in Literature and Language*, 6 (Summer 1964), pp. 226–54.

Guttman, Allen. *The Jewish Writer in America: Assimilation and The Crisis of Identity*. New York and London: Oxford University Press, 1971.

Hassan, Ihab. *Radical Innocence: Studies in the Contemporary American Novel*. Princeton, NJ: Princeton University Press, 1961. London: Harper & Row, 1963.

——'Saul Bellow: Five Faces of a Hero'. *Critique*, 3 (Summer 1960), pp. 28–36.

Howe, Irving (ed.). *Saul Bellow, Herzog: Text and Criticism*. New York: Viking Press, 1976.

Josipovici, Gabriel. *The World and the Book: A Study of Modern Fiction*. London: Macmillan, 1971. Stanford, Ca: Stanford University Press, 1971.

Kermode, Frank. 'Bellow's *Herzog*'. In Frank Kermode, *Continuities*. London: Routledge & Kegan Paul, 1968.

Klein, Marcus. *After Alienation: American Novels in Mid-Century*. Mountain View, Ca: World, 1962.

McConnell, Frank D. *Four Postwar American Novelists*. Chicago, Ill., and London: University of Chicago Press, 1977.

Malin, Irving. *Saul Bellow's Fiction*. Carbondale, Ill.: Southern Illinois University Press, 1969.

——(ed.). *Saul Bellow and the Critics*. New York: New York University Press, 1967. London: University of London Press, 1967.

Opdahl, Keith M. *The Novels of Saul Bellow*. University Park, Pa: Pennsylvania State University Press, 1967.

Rovit, Earl, *Saul Bellow*. Minneapolis, Minn.: University of Minnesota Press, 1967.

——(ed.). *Saul Bellow: A Collection of Critical Essays*. Englewood Cliffs, NJ: Prentice-Hall, 1975.

Salmagundi, 30 (Summer 1975). Saul Bellow Special Number.

Scheer-Schazler, Brigitte. *Saul Bellow*. New York: Ungar, 1972.

Schraepen, Edmond. *Comedy in Saul Bellow's Work*. Liège, Belgium: University of Liège Press, 1975.

——(ed.). *Saul Bellow and His Work*. Brussels: Vrije Universiteit Brussel, 1978.

Scott, Nathan A. *Three American Moralists: Mailer, Bellow, Trilling*. Notre Dame, Ind.: University of Notre Dame Press, 1973.

Tanner, Tony. *Saul Bellow*. Edinburgh: Oliver & Boyd, 1965. Reprinted by Chips Bookshop, USA, 1978.

DATE DUE

DATE DUE			
JAN 1 2 1983			
NOV 1 7 1988			
JUL 0 5 1994			
MAY 3 0 2000			
GAYLORD			PRINTED IN U.S.A.